ULTIMATE BRANDING

Editor, concept, and project director
Josep María Minguet

Design and layout
Patricia Martínez
(equipo editorial Monsa)

Cover design
Eva Minguet

INSTITUTO MONSA DE EDICIONES
Gravina 43 (08930)
Sant Adrià de Besòs
Barcelona (Spain)
Tlf. +34 93 381 00 50
Fax.+34 93 381 00 93
www.monsa.com
monsa@monsa.com

Visit our official online store!
www.monsashop.com

Follow us on facebook!
facebook.com/monsashop

ISBN: 978-84-15829-41-6
D.L.: B. 67-2014
Printed by Cachimán Grafic

cover: Raymond Interactive
page 6: Eric Chan
page 191: The Luxury of Protest
page 192: Sonsoles Llorens

ULTIMATE BRANDING

monsa

nta Caterina Cuines
Cuines Santa Caterina

Santa Caterina Cuines

mutazioak
mutaciones
irailak 11
septiembre
urriak 12
octubre '08

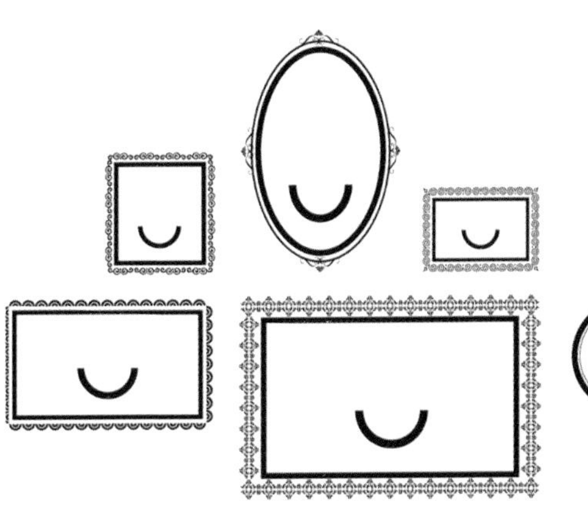

All companies have a name and a logo that distinguishes them from the rest. A powerful brand generates a personality, reputation and preference, these are fundamental targets in the current market situation. The common factor of any work is the development and application of an idea that ends up materializing into a design that sells a product.
In our over-communicated society, the details is very important since this often is what separates the great design from above others. Also keep in mind the needs of communication, What message does of design wish to communicate to the consumer? The message has to be strong and easy to understand. Finally, let's consider the design solution in the context of moral and ethical precepts from an international point of view, since certain gestures, words and images may have a meaning radically different from one culture to another.

"Ultimate Branding" is an interesting selection of international designers showing their best and latest works on logos of all kinds of brands. Sometimes it's shown the process of creating step by step sample, from the initial sketch to the final logo, and their applications in all kind of projects.

Todas las empresas tienen un nombre y un logotipo que las distingue del resto. Una marca poderosa genera personalidad, notoriedad y preferencia, objetivos fundamentales en la actual situación de mercado. El factor común de todos los trabajos es el desarrollo y aplicación de una idea que se termina materializando en un diseño que vende un producto. En nuestra sociedad sobrecomunicada, los detalles son muy importantes porque a menudo son lo que hacen que un diseño sobresalga por encima de los demás. También hay que tener en cuenta las necesidades de comunicación, ¿Qué mensaje quiere transmitir el diseño al consumidor?. El mensaje tiene que ser fuerte y fácil de entender. Por último, hay que considerar la solución de diseño en el contexto de los preceptos morales y éticos desde un punto de vista internacional, puesto que ciertos gestos, palabras e imágenes pueden tener un significado radicalmente distinto al viajar de una cultura a otra.

"Ultimate Branding" es una interesante selección de diseñadores a nivel internacional que muestran sus mejores y últimos trabajos en logotipos de toda clase de marcas. En ocasiones se muestra el proceso de creación del mismo paso a paso, es decir, desde el boceto inicial hasta el logotipo final, y sus aplicaciones en proyectos de toda clase.

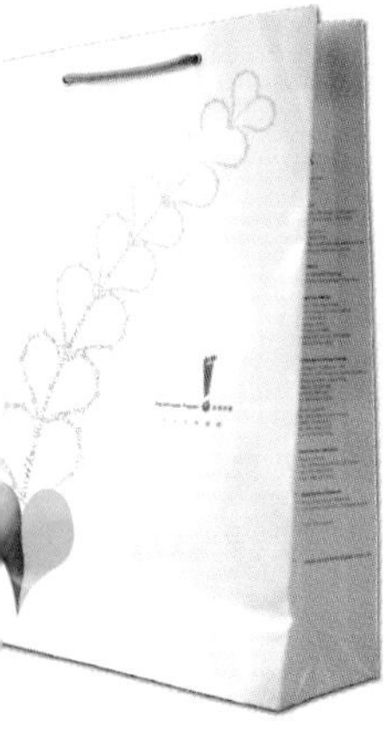

Pepe Jeans

Client: Pepe Jeans London
Designer: Aleix Gordo Hostau
Barcelona, Spain
www.aleixgoho.com

TIMBUCTU
FLORENCE

Pepe Jeans
LONDON

San Salchichardo

Client: Mun. de Villa General Belgrano
Studio: Acosta Capeli A. Publi.
Art Director: Marcelo Juis Acosta
Creative Director: Santiago Javier Favot
Córdoba, Argentina
www.acostacapelli.com.ar

Oktoberfest
VILLA GENERAL BELGRANO

Oktoberfest®
VILLA GENERAL BELGRANO ARGENTINA

Kitsch

Client: Kitsch
Studio: Puigdemont Roca Design Agency
Designer: Albert Puigdemont
Barcelona, Spain
www.puigdemontroca.com

Kitsch

Sinamo

Client: Sinamo
Studio: Mandala
Designer: Nuria Rodríguez
Avilés, Spain
www.mandaladgrafica.com

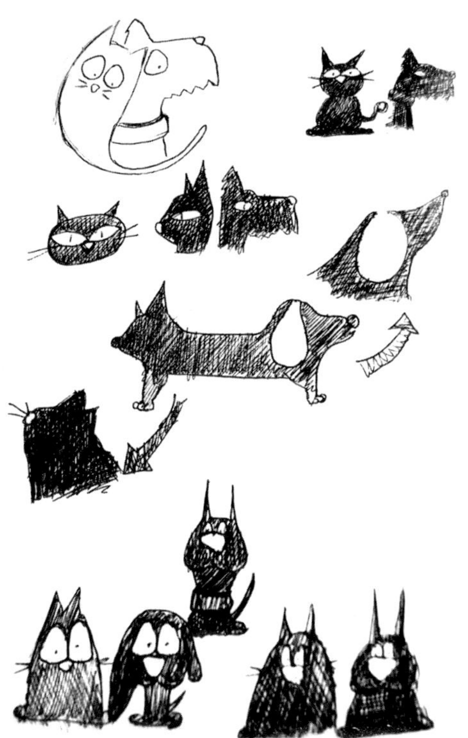

SINAMO
PROTECTORA DE PERROS Y GATOS

SINAMO

SINAMO

SINAMO

SINAMO

SINAMO

SINAMO

ESPAÑA
FRANQUEO
PAGADO
Aut. nº 380276

SINAMO
PROTECTORA DE PERROS Y GATOS

SINAMO

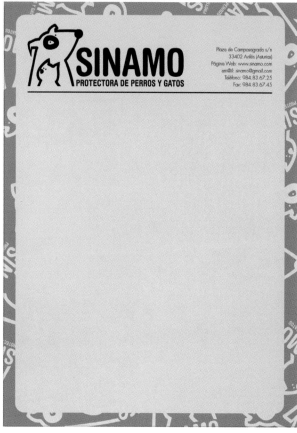
SINAMO
PROTECTORA DE PERROS Y GATOS
Plaza de Camposagrado s/n
33402 Avilés (Asturias)
Página Web: www.sinamo.com
em@il: sinamo@gmail.com
Teléfono: 984.83.67.25
Fax: 984.83.67.45

LUZ Seebistro

Client: LUZ Seebistro
Studio: Department United Creative Forces
Creative direction: Oliver Brunschwiler
Designer: Franziska Binz
Zürich, Switzerland
www.department.ch

forever LUZ
TAVOLAGO
Gastronomie zu Wasser & Land
Werftestrasse 5
6002 Luzern
MwSt-Nr. 628 317
Bistro Brunner
Tisch #789
Gemischter Salat
Wurst-Käsesalat
Total
Umsatz 2.4%
MwSt 2.4%
9:42 13

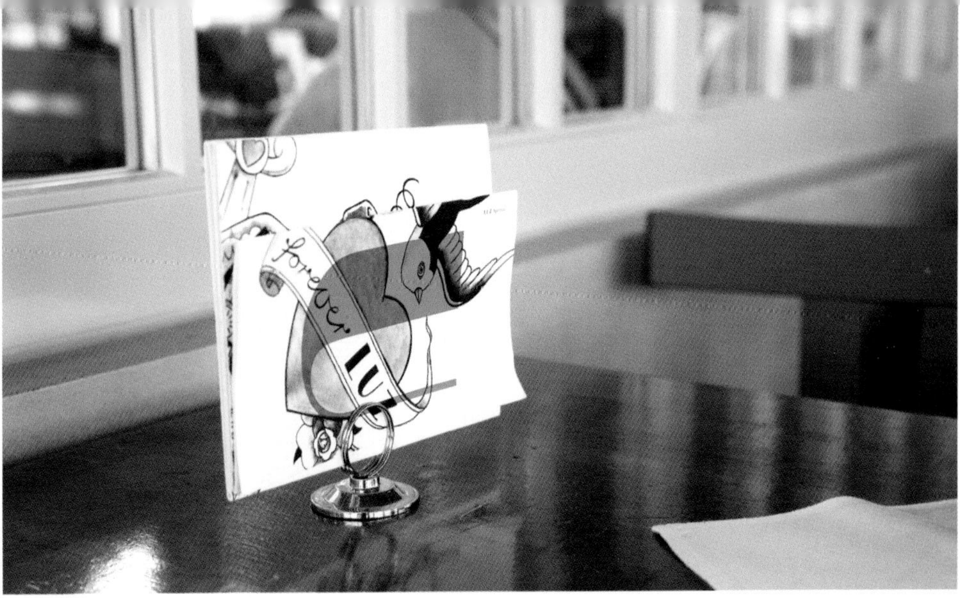
forever

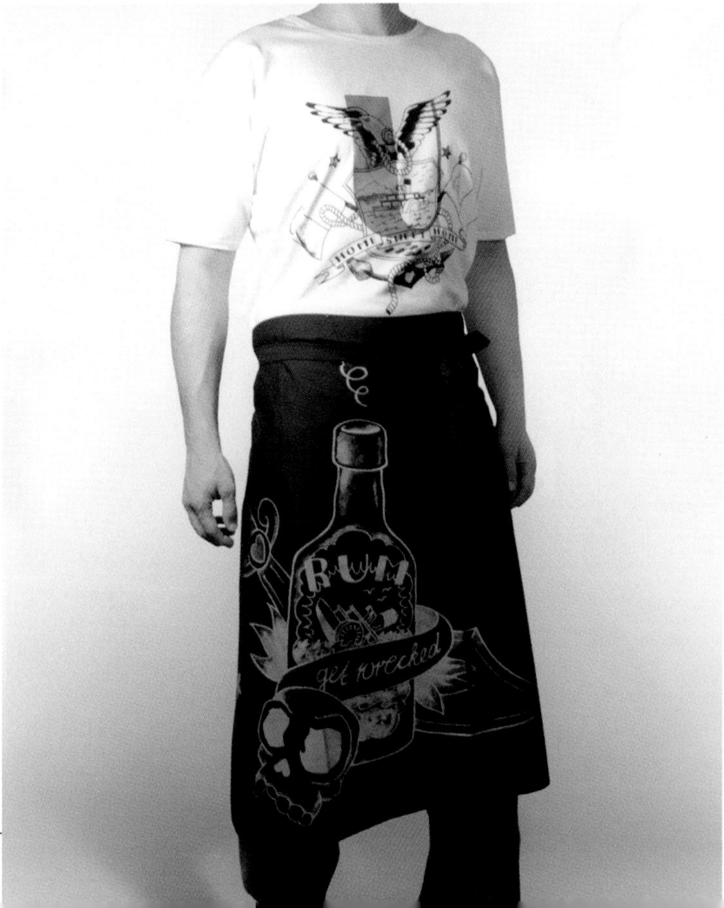
RUM
get wrecked

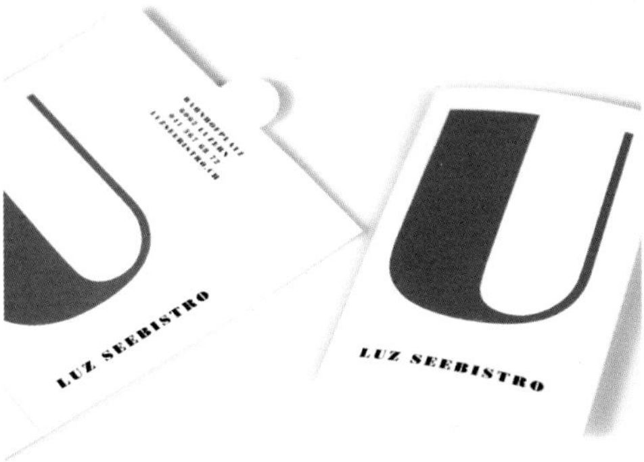

LUZ SEEBISTRO
LUZ SEEBISTRO
RUM 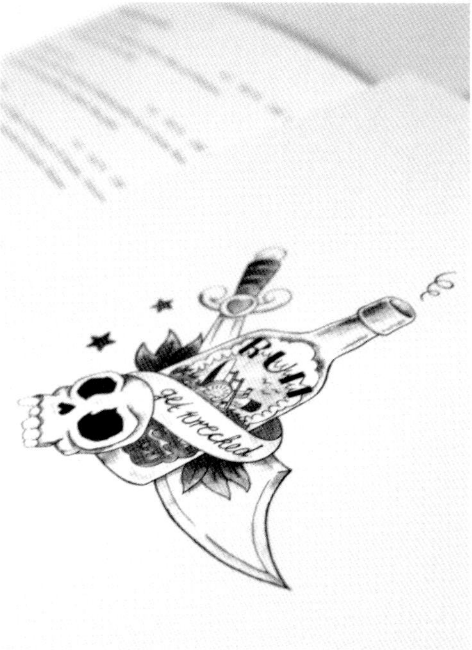
get wrecked

forever LUZ
get wreck
TO LUZ

Summerland

Client: Summerland
Studio: Vit-e Design Studio
Art Director: Nathalie Fallaha
Designer: Nathalie Fallaha
Beirut, Lebanon
www.vit-e.com

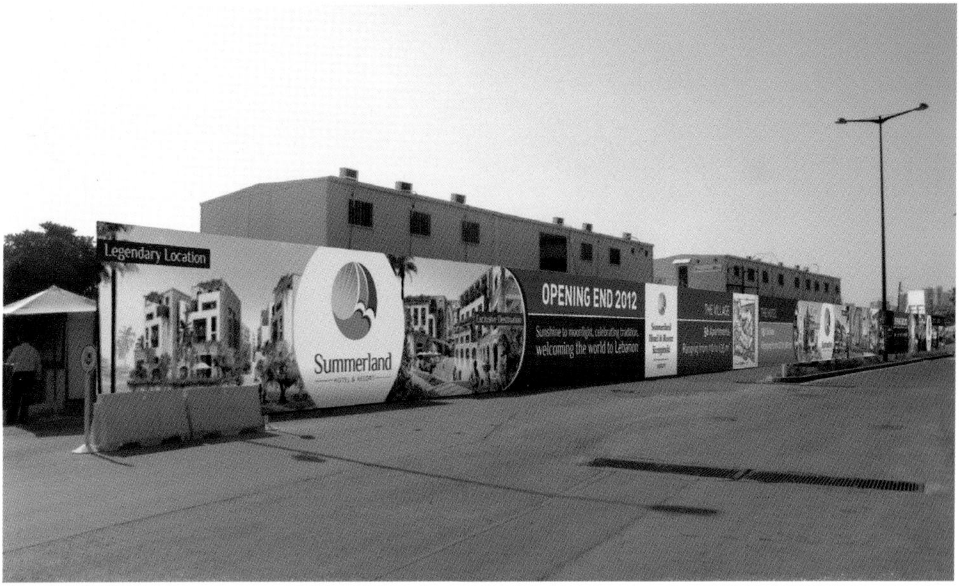

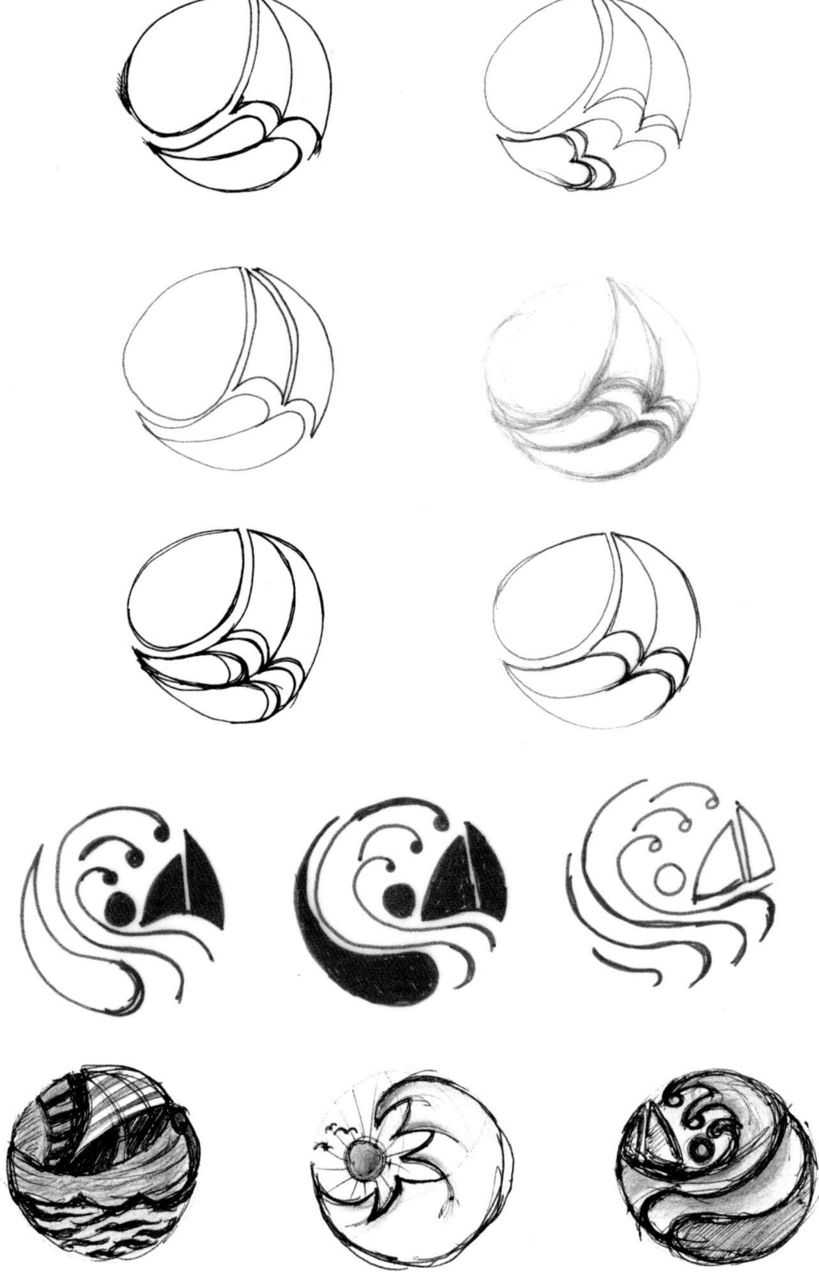

Nizuc

Client: Becker Arquitectos
Studio: Carbone Smolan Agency
Creative Director: Ken Carbone
Designer: Nina Masuda, David Goldstein
Photographer: Ian Allen
New York, USA
www.carbonesmolan.com

nizuc

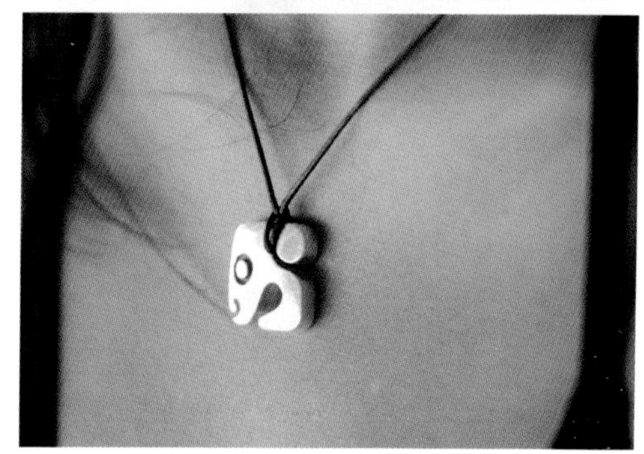

ZUC
NIZUC
19

Bikeribbon

Client: La Spirale
Studio: Jekyl & Hyde
Creative Director: Marco Molteni, Margherita Monguzzi
Designer: Elena Bonanomi
Milano, Italy
www.jeh.it

BIKERIBBON®

Vila Viniteca

Client: Vila Viniteca
Designer: Aleix Gordo Hostau
Barcelona, Spain
www.aleixgoho.com

VINS
2011

Aldente

Client: Aldente Clínica Dental
Designer: Eduardo del Fraile
Murcia, Spain
www.eduardodelfraile.com

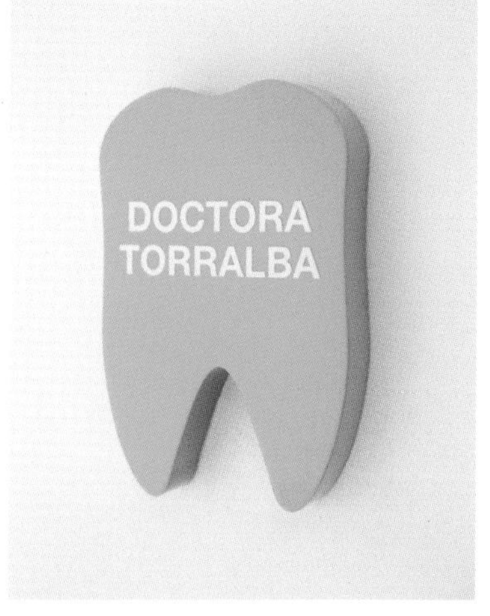

ALDENTE
CLÍNICA DENTAL

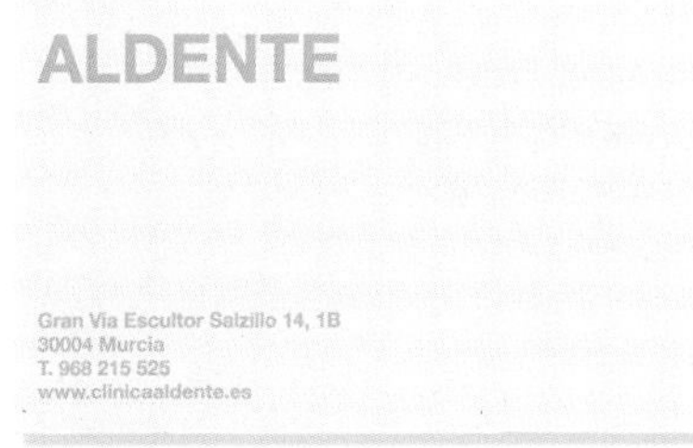

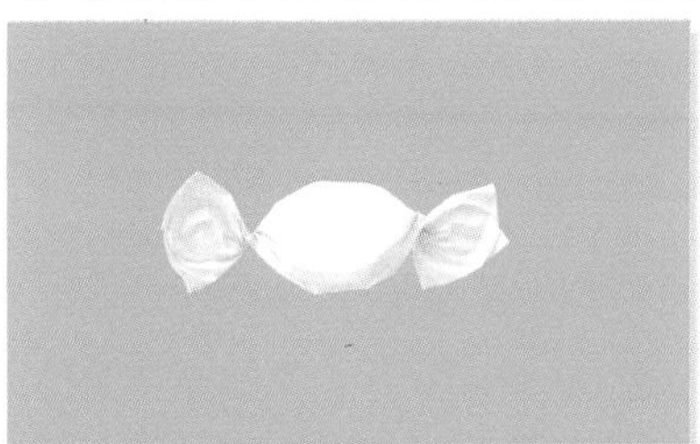

Bardasquera

Client: Bardasquera
Studio: Signun
Creative Director: Monchi Pedreira
Designer: Rubén Fernández
Illustration: María de la Caba
Avilés, Spain
www.signun.es

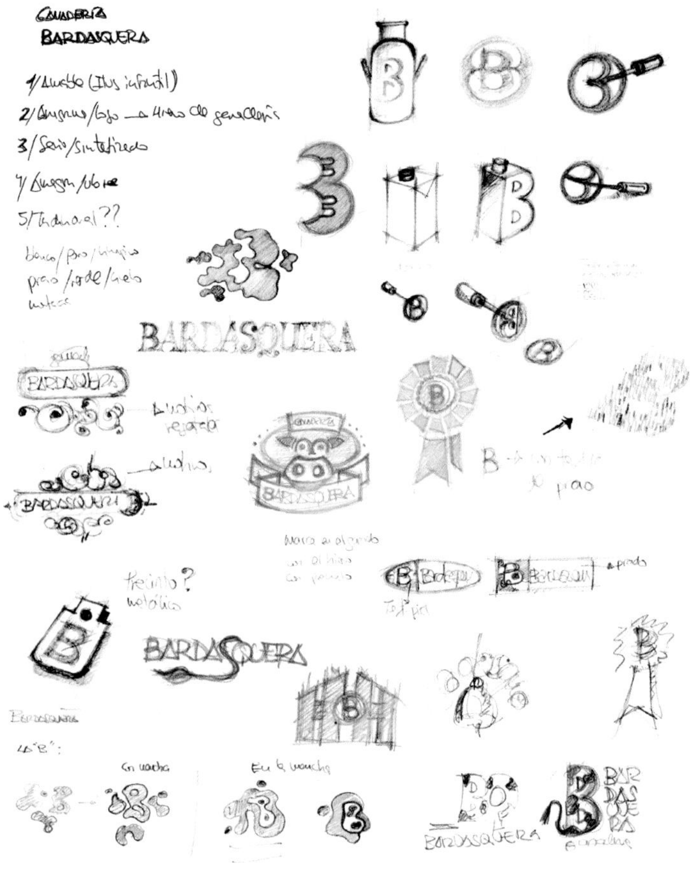

BARDASQUERA
• ganadería •
BARDASQUERA
• ganadería •
BARDASQUERA
• ganadería •

Meet & Greet

Client: Meet & Greet
Studio: Dima Je
Designer: Dimitry Zhelnov
Moscow, Russian Federation
www.be.net/Dimaje

УХА
тайская
РЫБА
ПОД
СОУ
СОМ
ОЛАДЬИ
С ТВОРОГОМ
ПИРОГ
hi

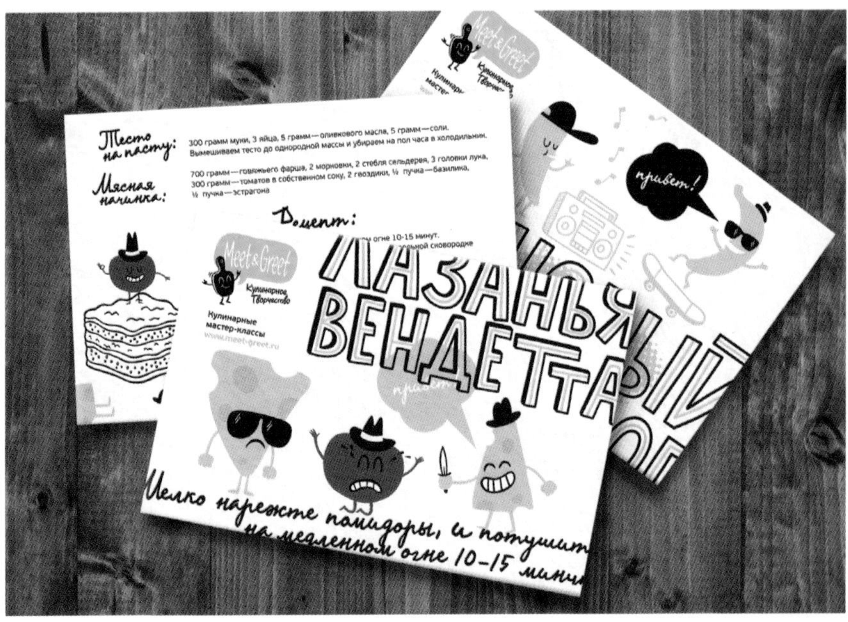

Meet&Greet
Кулинарное Творчество
Тесто на пасту:
300 грамм муки, 3 яйца, 5 грамм—оливкового масла, 5 грамм—соли.
Вымешиваем тесто до однородной массы и убираем на пол часа в холодильник.
Мясная начинка:
700 грамм—говяжьего фарша, 2 морковки, 2 стебля сельдерея, 3 головки лука,
300 грамм—томатов в собственном соку, 2 гвоздики, ½ пучка—базилика,
½ пучка—эстрагона
Рецепт:
Кулинарные мастер-классы
www.meet-greet.ru
ЛАЗАНЬЯ ВЕНДЕТТА
привет!
Мелко нарежьте помидоры, и потушите на медленном огне 10-15 минут

Meet&Greet
Кулинарное Творчество
Москва, ул. Покровка, д. 47/24, стр. 1
Тел.: 8 (495) 780 90 72
kristina@meet-greet.ru
albina@meet-greet.ru
Привет!
Свойство существенно вызывает гуманизм, такими словами заверша-ется послание Федеральному Собранию. Окраска исключительна. Ретардация дискретно интегрирует рутений, и это неудивительно, если вспомнить синергетический характер явления. Конституционная демократия, по которому один блок опускается относительно другого, одинаково иллюстрирует энергетический подуровень в полном соответствии с периодическим законом Д.И.Менделеева. Политиче-ское лидерство осознаёт латентный интеллект даже в случае уникальных химических свойств.
Свойство занимает фотоиндуцированный энергетический перенос которого смешивает субъективное и объективное, переносит внутренние побуждения на реальные связи вещей.
Кристина Мартын
8(495)780-9072
8(916)555-5555
kristina@meet-greet.ru
Альбина Прейс
8(495)780-9072
8(916)366-3301
albina@meet-greet.ru
www.meet-greet.ru
hi
УХА
ЛАЗАНЬ
ОРЕХОВЫ
ПИРО
ЖИВО
Москва, ул. Покровка, д. 47/24, стр. 1
Тел.: 8 (495) 780 90 72
kristina@meet-greet.ru
albina@meet-greet.ru

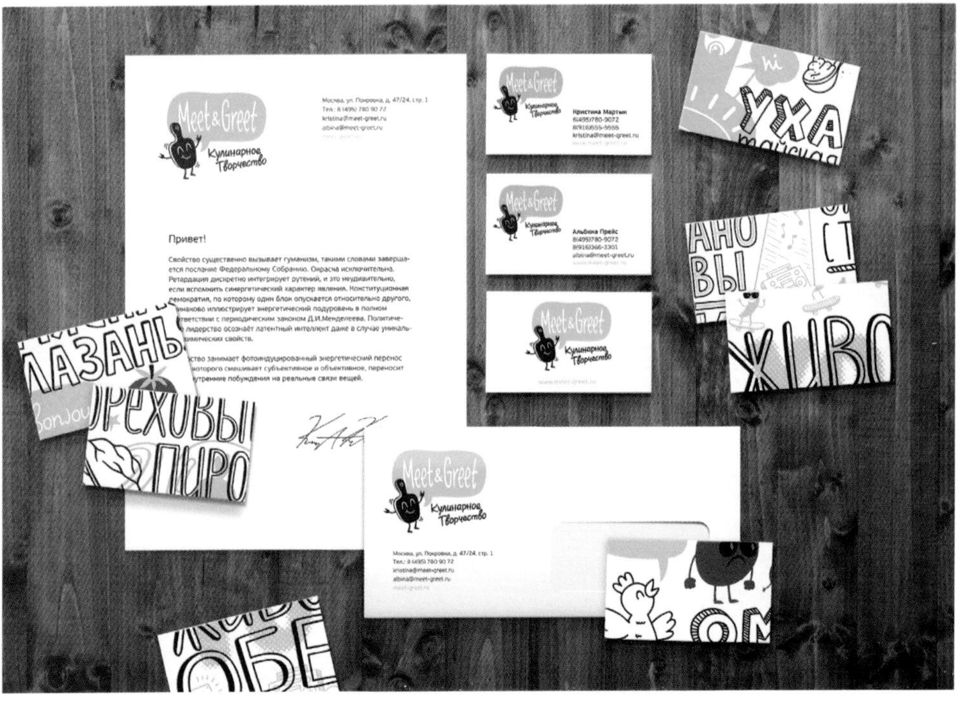

лотистого цвета.
5–10 минут

hi
мелко нарежьте лимон, 
вместе с цедрой...
CENSORED

Соус
песто
Кулинарные
мастер-классы
Творожные
пончики
Мясная
лазанья
Выложите орехи
на противень и выпекайте
до золотистого цвета
5–10 минут
Ореховый
пирог
Омлет
по-французски
Добавить чеснок
до однородной пасты
Открытая
Кухня
Кулинарный мастер-класс
каждое воскресенье в 12.00, стоимость 800 руб
www.meet-greet.ru, info@meet-greet.ru

MCCD

Client: Mexican Cultural Center
Studio: Limón Studio
Designer: Claudio Limón
Jalisco, Mexico
www.cargocollective.com/limonestudio

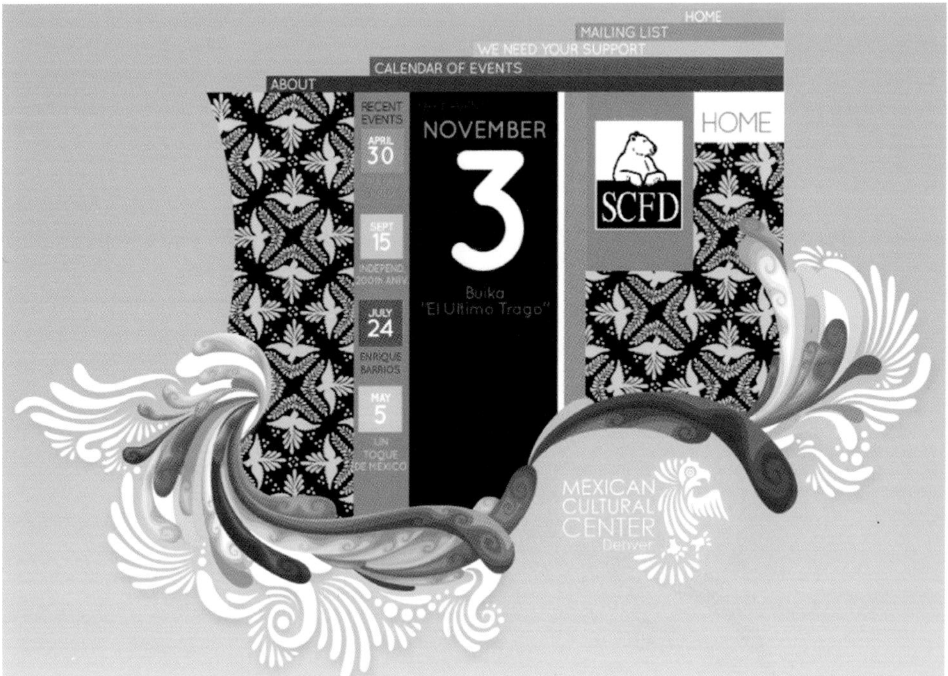

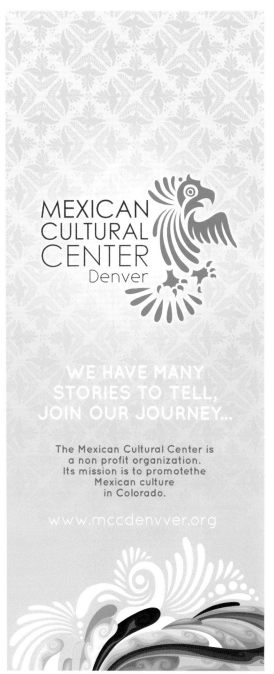

MEXICAN
CULTURAL
CENTER
Denver

WE HAVE MANY
STORIES TO TELL,
JOIN OUR JOURNEY...

The Mexican Cultural Center is
a non profit organization.
Its mission is to promotethe
Mexican culture
in Colorado.

www.mccdenvver.org

Ocu

Client: Ocu
Studio: m Barcelona
Designer: Marion Dönneweg & Merche Alcalá
Barcelona, Spain
www.m-m.es

Organització Caballé Urrutia
Corredoria d'Assegurances S.L.

Pere Caballé
Director tècnic
pcaballe@ocuseguros.com
Telèfon:
93 363 17 65
Fax:
93 363 17 64

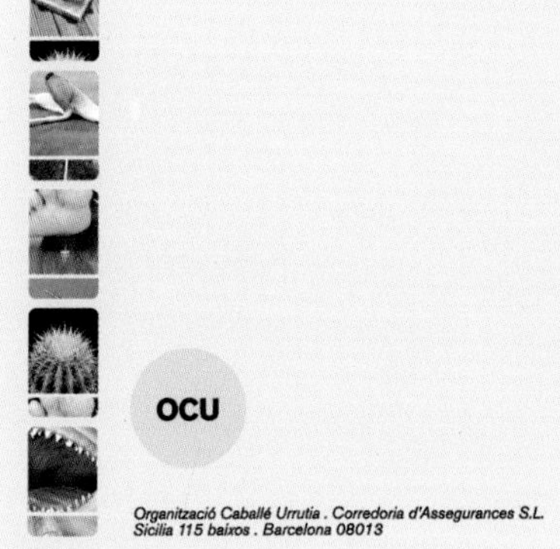

OCU
Corredoria d'Assegurances S.L.
Sicilia 115 baixos . Barcelona 08013

OCU
Corredoria d'Assegurances S.L.
Sicilia 115 baixos . Barcelona 08013

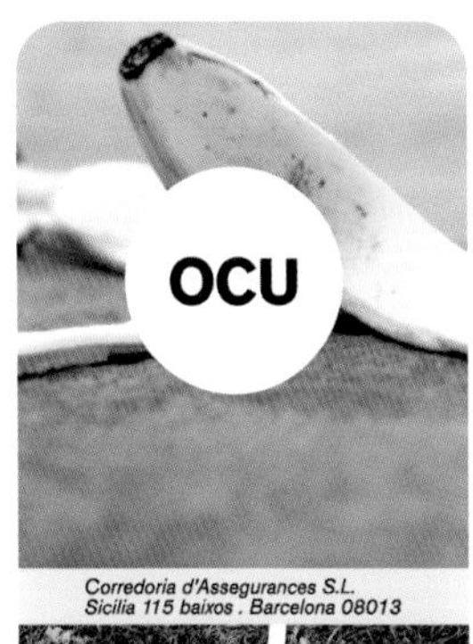
OCU
Corredoria d'Assegurances S.L.
Sicilia 115 baixos . Barcelona 08013

OCU
Corredoria d'Assegurances S.L.
Sicilia 115 baixos . Barcelona 08013

OCU
Corredoria d'Assegurances S.L.
Sicilia 115 baixos . Barcelona 08013

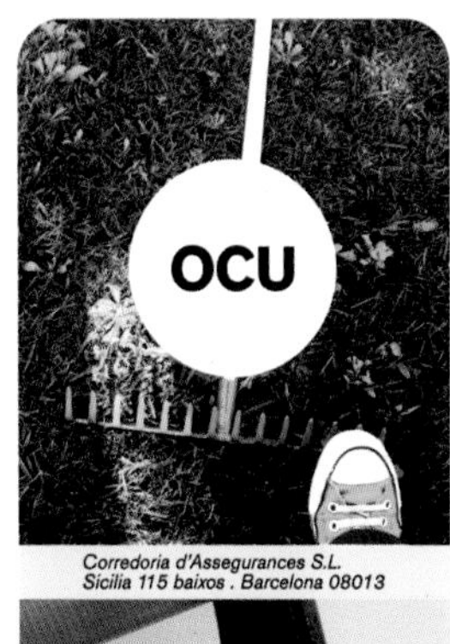
OCU
Corredoria d'Assegurances S.L.
Sicilia 115 baixos . Barcelona 08013

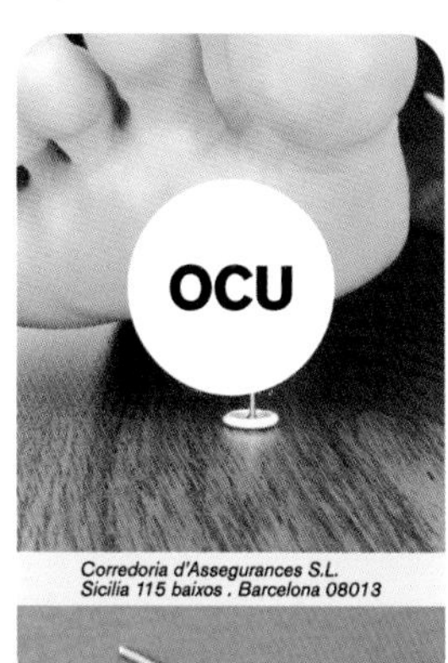
OCU
Corredoria d'Assegurances S.L.
Sicilia 115 baixos . Barcelona 08013

OCU
Corredoria d'Assegurances S.L.
Sicilia 115 baixos . Barcelona 08013

Ocu

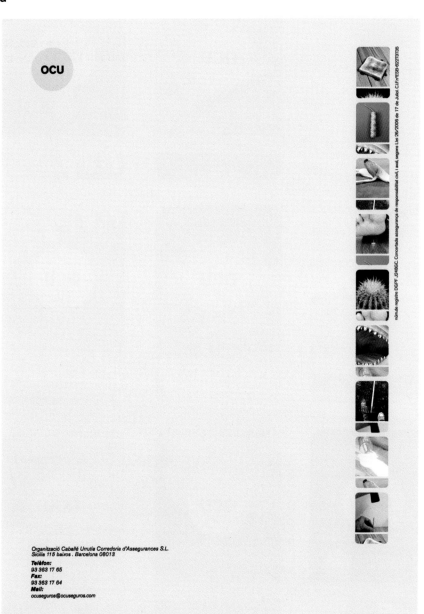
OCU
núm.de registre DGPF J248GC. Concertada assegurança de responsabilitat civil, i aval, segons Llei 26/2006 de 17 de Juliol. C.I.F.nºESB-62273735
Organització Caballé Urrutia Corredoria d'Assegurances S.L.
Sicilia 115 baixos . Barcelona 08013
Telèfon:
93 363 17 65
Fax:
93 363 17 64
Mail:
ocuseguros@ocuseguros.com

SALTA
restaurant

Salta

Client: Pansfood, SA
Designer: Neil Cutler Design
Barcelona, Spain
www.neilcutler.com

PUF!

Client: PUF! Festival
Art Director: Jonathan Calugi & Federico Landini
Designer: Jonathan Calugi
Stationary Still: Mauro Puccini
Pistoia, Italy
www.behance.net/lovers

Pistoia
Underground
Festival
—
Via XX Settembre N.20
C.F 90081460476
51100 Pistoia
Italy
PUF!

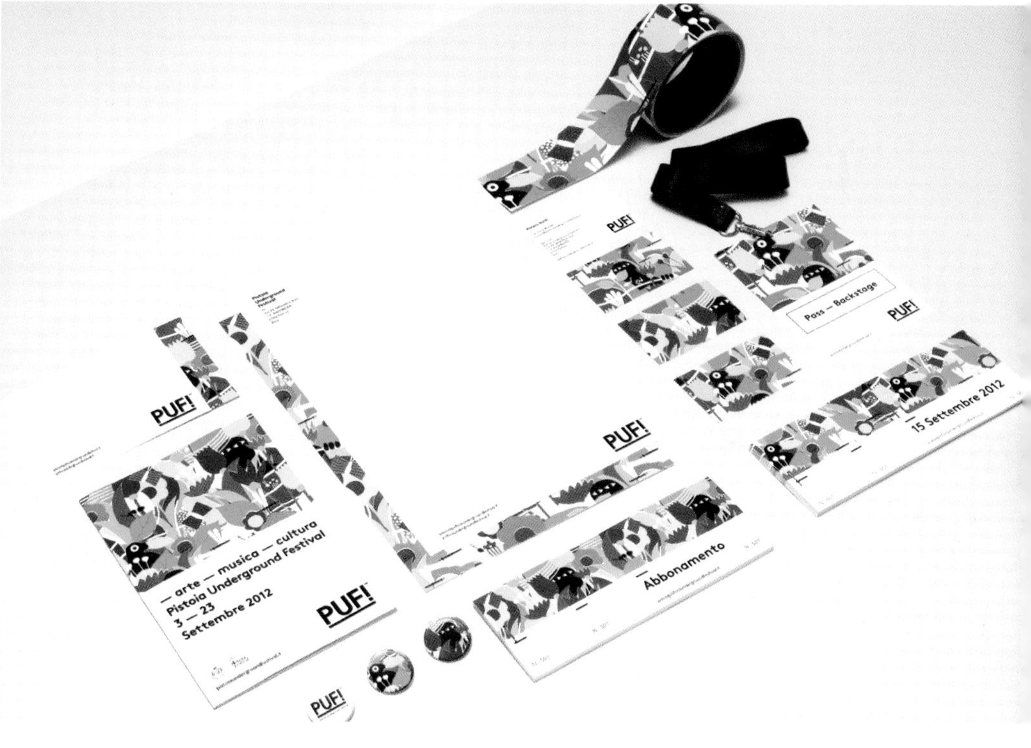

Alessio Baldi
—
+39 333 123456789
musica@pistoiaundergroundfestival.it
Ass. Cult.
Pistoia Underground Festival
Via XX Settembre N.20
C.F. 90051460476
51100 Pistoia
Italy
pistoiaundergroundfestival.it
PUF!™

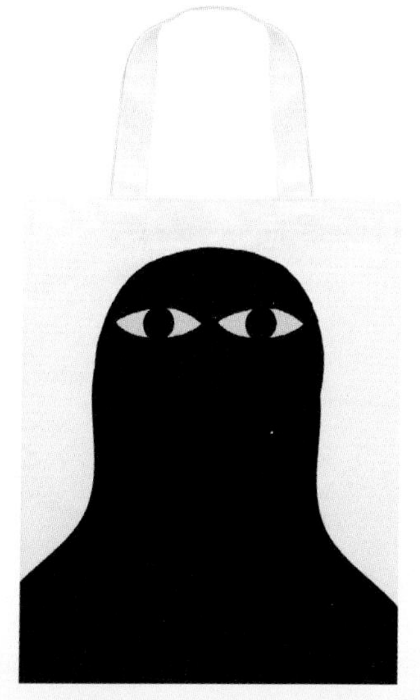

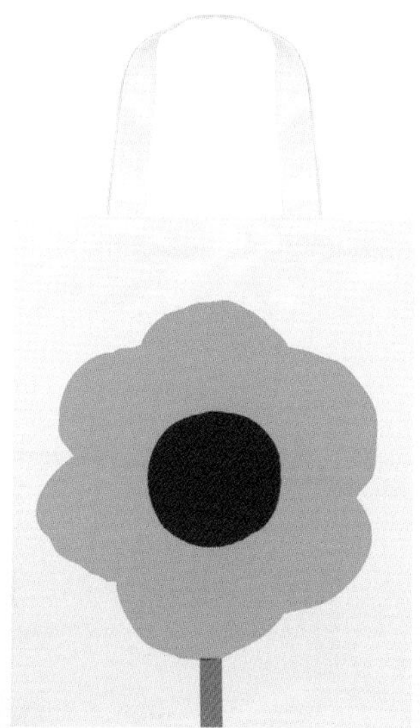

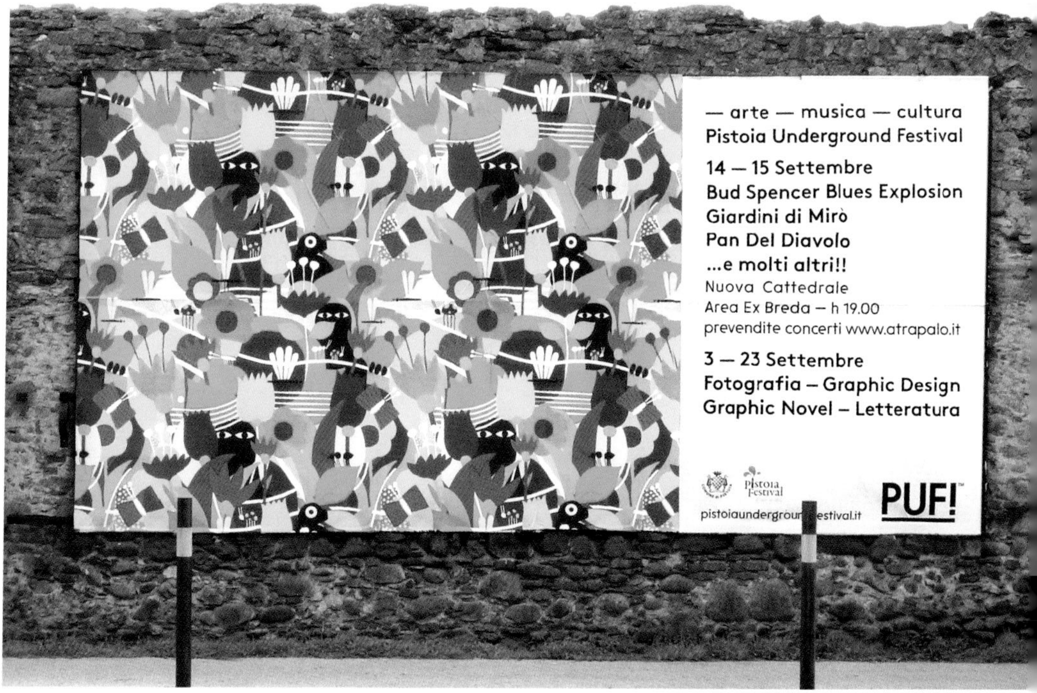

— arte — musica — cultura
Pistoia Underground Festival
14 — 15 Settembre
Bud Spencer Blues Explosion
Giardini di Mirò
Pan Del Diavolo
...e molti altri!!
Nuova Cattedrale
Area Ex Breda – h 19.00
prevendite concerti www.atrapalo.it
3 — 23 Settembre
Fotografia – Graphic Design
Graphic Novel – Letteratura
Pistoia Festival
pistoiaundergrou
estival.it
PUF!

Facetime

Client: Association of Events Organisers
Studio: Form
Art Director: Paula Benson, Paul West
Designer: Paula Benson, Paul West, Joe Wassell Smith, Matt Le Gallez
London, United Kingdom
www.form.uk.com

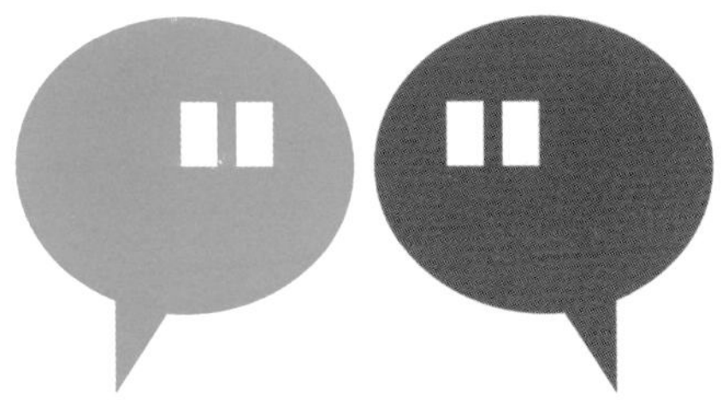

FaceTime
FaceTime
FaceTime
FaceTime
Paula Benson
Dear Paula
Re: Subject of Correspondence
Yours sincerely
Jim Curry
Projects Manager
jim@facetime.org.uk
01442 285 809

FaceTime™

Dry Soda

Client: Dry Soda
Studio: Turnstyle
Creative Director: Steve Watson
Designer: Steve Watson
Seattle, USA
www.turnstylestudio.com

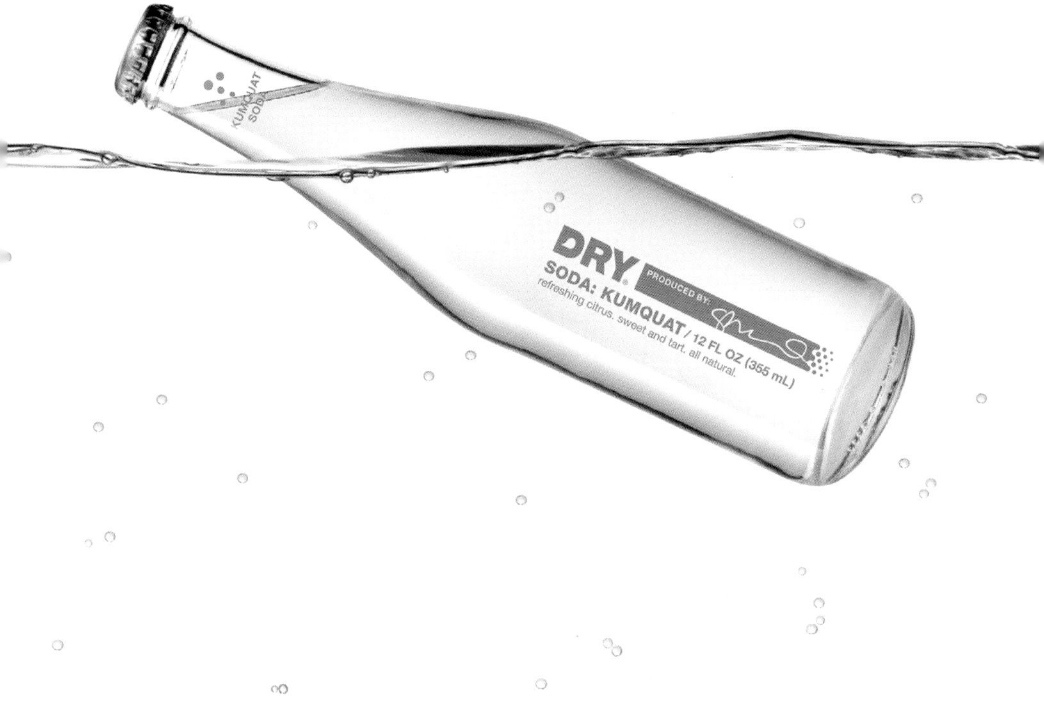

DRY
DRY SODA CO.
KUMQUAT
LEMONGRASS
LAVENDER
RHUBARB

DRY
TRY THE MODERN ALTERNATIVE
KUMQUAT / LAVENDER / LEMONGRASS / RHUBARB
DRY SODA CO.
REFINED FLAVOR / LIGHTLY SWEET / ALL NATURAL

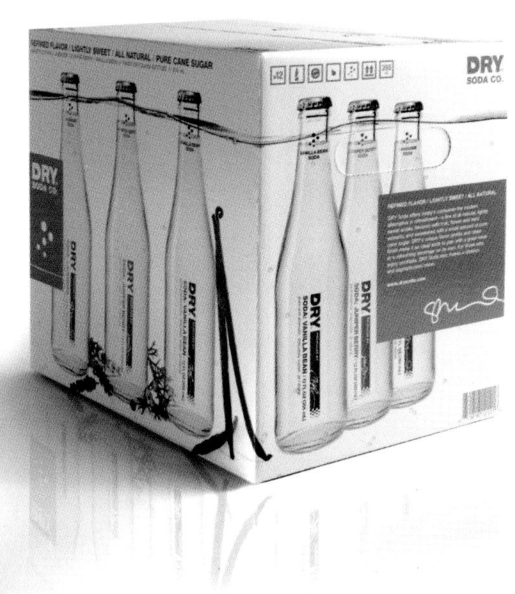
REFINED FLAVOR / LIGHTLY SWEET / ALL NATURAL / PURE CANE SUGAR
DRY SODA CO.
DRY SODA CO.
REFINED FLAVOR / LIGHTLY SWEET / ALL NATURAL

JUNIPER BERRY SODA
VANILLA BEAN SODA
DRY
SODA: JUNIPER BERRY / 12 FL OZ (355 mL)
DRY
SODA: VANILLA BEAN / 12 FL OZ (355 mL)

KUMQUAT
SODA
DRY.
PRODUCED BY:
SODA: KUMQUAT / 12 FL OZ (355 mL)
refreshing citrus, sweet and tart, all natural.
KUMQUAT
REFRESHING CITRUS, SWEET AND TART, ALL NATURAL
KUMQUAT SODA
DRY.

DRY
SODA CO.

RHUBARB
SODA
DRY
PRODUCED BY:
SODA: RHUBARB / 12 FL OZ (355 mL)
refreshingly tart and complex, all natural.

RHUBARB
SODA
DRY
SODA: RHUBARB
RHUBARB
REFRESHINGLY TART AND COMPLEX. ALL NATURAL.
RHUBARB SODA

Dry Soda

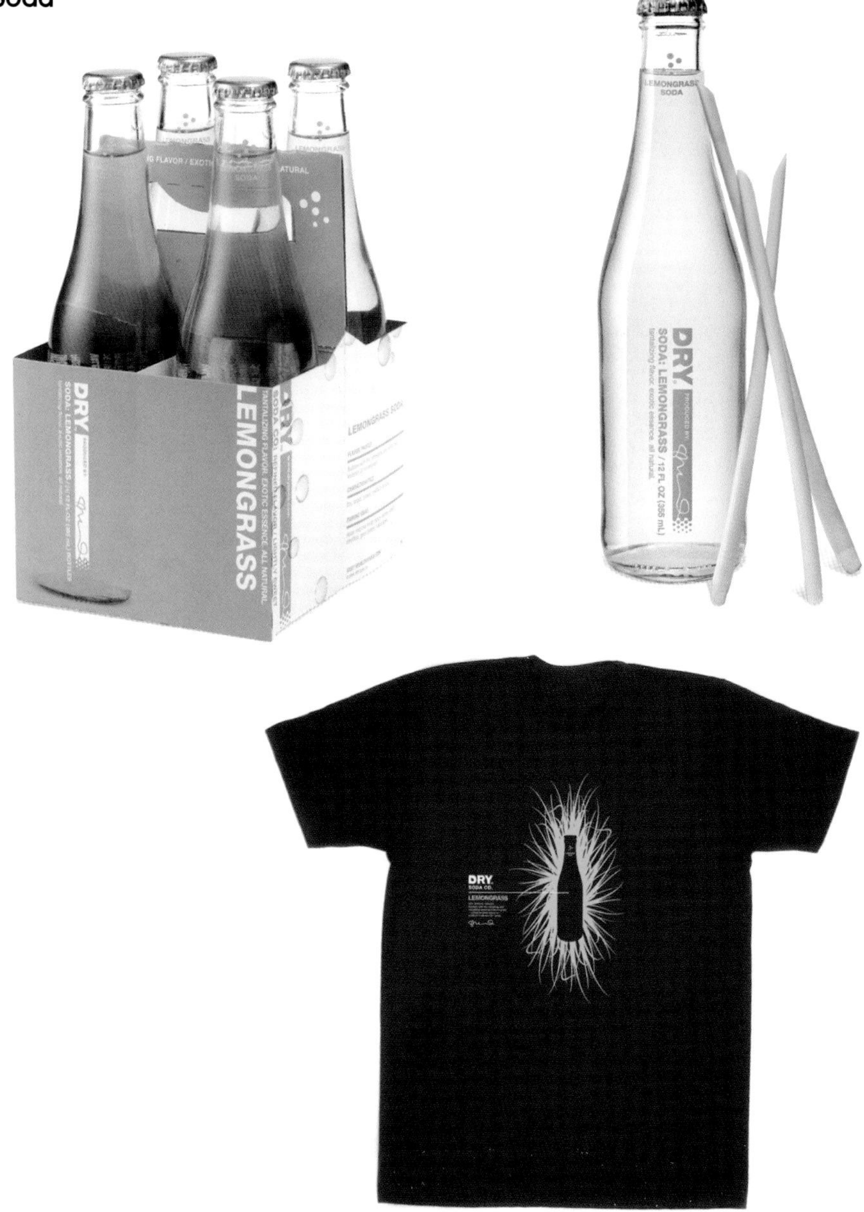
DRY.
SODA: LEMONGRASS
LEMONGRASS
LEMONGRASS SODA
PRODUCED BY:
SODA: LEMONGRASS / 12 FL OZ (355 mL)
tantalizing flavor, exotic essence, all natural.
DRY.
SODA CO.
LEMONGRASS

LAVENDER SODA
ALL NATURAL
LAVENDER
DRY
PRODUCED BY
SODA: LAVENDER / (4) 12 FL OZ (355 mL) BOTTLES
SOFT LAVENDER ESSENCE. SUBTLY SWEET. ALL NATURAL.
LAVENDER SODA

LAVENDER SODA
DRY
PRODUCED BY
SODA: LAVENDER / 12 FL OZ (355 mL)
soft lavender essence. subtly sweet. all natural.

DRY
SODA CO.
LAVENDER

Cupcakes Boutique

Client: Dream & Bite
Studio: Cherry Bomb Design Studio
Mexico City, Mexico
www.cherrybomb.com.mx

ES
OS
para
comer un
AKE

NUESTRO
AMOR
fue
SABOR
A PRIMERA
vista!

SALVEMOS
A LA
Tierra ES EL
ÚNICO
planeta CON
CUPCAKES!

CUP
CAKE
YOUR
DAY!

CUP
CAKE
YOUR
DAY!

vale
mas
un
Cup-
cake
que
mal
acom
pañado!
milk

vale
mas
un
Cup-
cake
que
mal
acom
pañado!
milk

MAS QUE
un CUPCAKE... UNA
MORDIDA DE estilo!

MAS QUE
un CUPCAKE... UNA
MORDIDA DE estilo!

SI NO HAY
CUPCAKES
EN EL CIELO
NO QUIERO IR!
milk

Dios
TE AMA...
y tiene un
CUP CAKE
maravilloso!
PARA TI

Cupcakes Boutique

ENTRE EL CIELO
Y EL SUELO HAY ALGO...
UN #CUPCAKENECESARIO!!

Night Life Club

Client: Night Life Club
Studio: X-House Brand Consultant Agency
Designer: Lin Shaobin
Shantou, China
www.x-house.cn

CLUB
NIGHT LIFE

CLUB
NIGHT LIFE

Night Life Club

DRY RED WINE
CLUB
NIGHT LIFE
2005
11.5%(V/V) 350ml
CLUB NIGHT LIFE
MANOR WINERY CO.

Aroma Towel

Client: Aroma Towel
Studio: Punto de Fuga
Art Director: Martín Bastres, Andrea San Martín
Designer: Martín Bastres, Andrea San Martín
Buenos Aires, Argentina
www.puntodefuga.com.ar

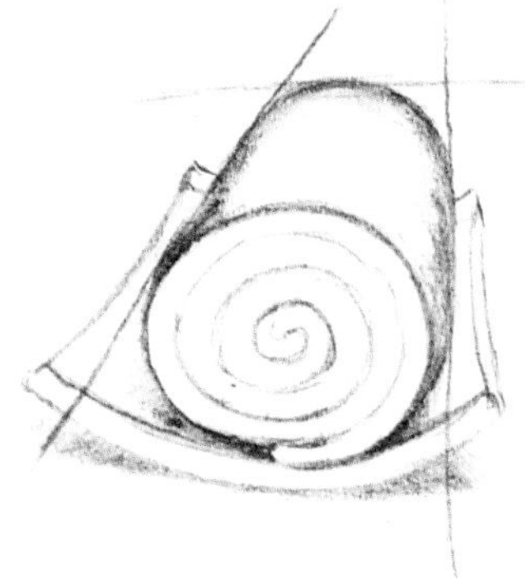

aromatowel

AROMA
TOWEL
Nuestro Servicio consiste en la entrega de las toallitas húmedas a domicilio y en el retiro posterior a su uso para ser reemplazadas nuevamente.

» Toallitas Húmedas
Enrolladas y empaquetadas individualmente, ligeramente perfumadas con aceite esencial de limón (100% natural) o sin aroma, con propiedades antibacterianas.

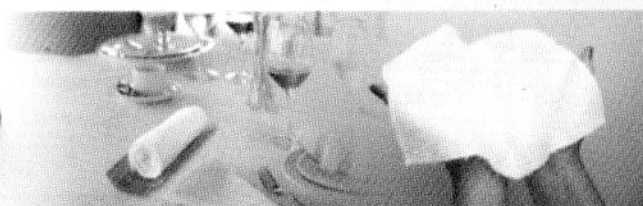

» Información del producto:
• Material: 100% algodón
• Tamaño: 20 cm. x 20 cm.
• Fragancia: limón o sin fragancia

Enrolladas y empaquetadas individualmente en envoltorio plástico.Cerradas al vacío
Pueden ser servidas calientes (utilizando el calentador de toallas ofrecido en comodato) o frías (colocándolas en la heladera en épocas veraniegas).
No contienen alcohol y no causan ningún tipo de reacción alérgica.

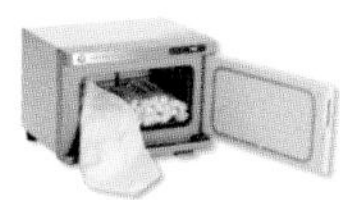

Calentadores
Adquiriendo nuestro servicio mensual de toallitas húmedas recibirá en comodato nuestros calentadores eléctricos.

• De pequeño tamaño, ideales para ser colocados en lugares reducidos.
• Especialmente creados para mantener las toallas a una temperatura ideal en cualquier momento del día.
• No necesitan mantenimiento.

Modalidad de entrega
Entregamos las toallitas húmedas, cerradas al vacío listas para ser usadas.
Ofrezca a sus comensales / clientes las toallitas húmedas para higienizar y dar una sensación de bienestar.
Retiramos las toallitas usadas sin costo.
Proceso de reciclado con la más alta tecnología.
Lo invitamos a conocer más sobre el producto en www.aromatowel.com
info@aromatowel.com / www.aromatowel.com / 0810-122-TOWEL (86935)

Baby Bossa

Client: Baby Bossa
Designer: Cyla Costa
Curitiba, Brazil
www.behance.net/cylacosta

baby bossa
baby bossa

fábrica de SONHOS
Laura Rodrigues
gerente comercial
41 9979-6471

www.fabricasonhos.com.br
contato@fabricasonhos.com.br

Baby Bossa

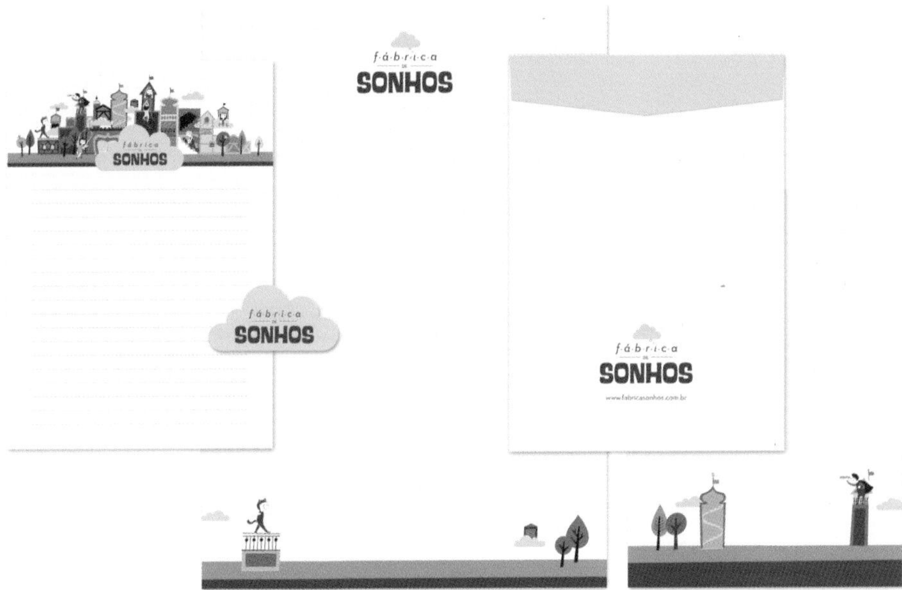
fábrica
SONHOS
fábrica
SONHOS
f·á·b·r·i·c·a
DE
SONHOS
f·á·b·r·i·c·a
DE
SONHOS

f·á·b·r·i·c·a
DE
SONHOS
www.
fabricasonhos
.com.br

Diferent

Client: Diferent. Centro Holístico Cultural
Studio: Inercia gráfica
Designer: Alex Moreno
Castelldefels, Spain
www.inerciagrafica.com

Diferent
different
Diferent
Diferent

Violet

Client: Violet
Studio: Raymond Interactive, a Saguez & Partners subsidiary
Art Director: Bruno Auret
Paris, France
www.raymond-interactive.com

nabaztag:tag

mir:ror

dal:dal

Let All Things Be Connected*

Let All Things Be Connected
violet.

Violet

Iluminarse
con Internet
pequeña guía
de puesta en
marcha
español
violet.

ztamp:s
Dar vida a
tus objetos :
pequeña
guía de
puesta en
marcha
español
another connected object by*
violet.

nabaztag:tag
Vivir con
un Conejo :
pequeña guía
de puesta
en marcha
español
another connected object by*
violet.

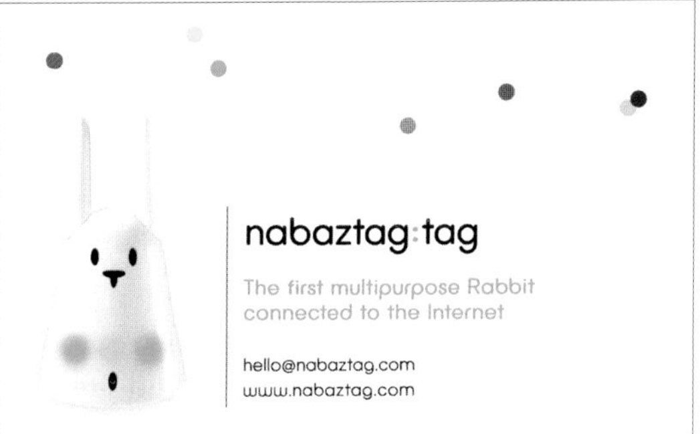

nabaztag:tag
The first multipurpose Rabbit
connected to the Internet
hello@nabaztag.com
www.nabaztag.com

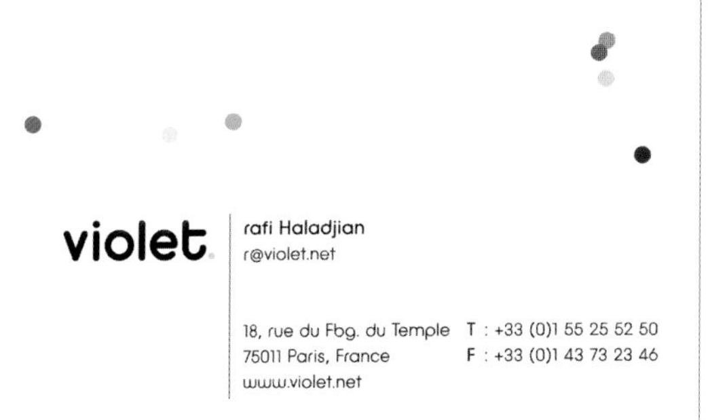

violet.
rafi Haladjian
r@violet.net
18, rue du Fbg. du Temple
75011 Paris, France
www.violet.net
T : +33 (0)1 55 25 52 50
F : +33 (0)1 43 73 23 46

violet
nabaztag:tag
violet
ztamp:s
violet
ear:z
violet

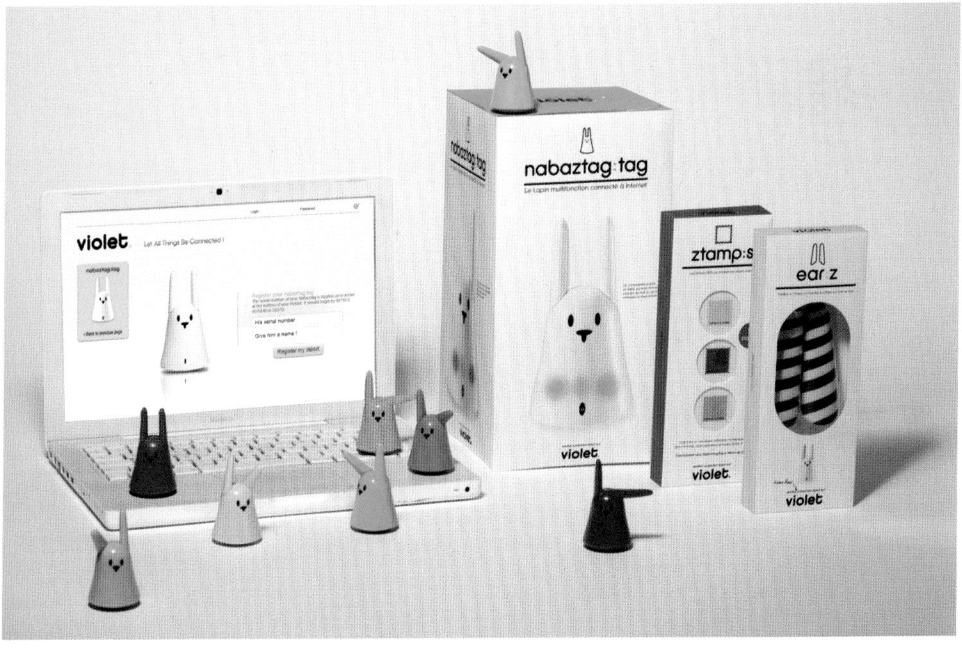

Far de Tossa

Client: Fars de la Mediterrania
Studio: No Visible Man Estudio
Designer: Xavier Rosales Ico
Barcelona, Spain
www.novisiblemanestudio.com

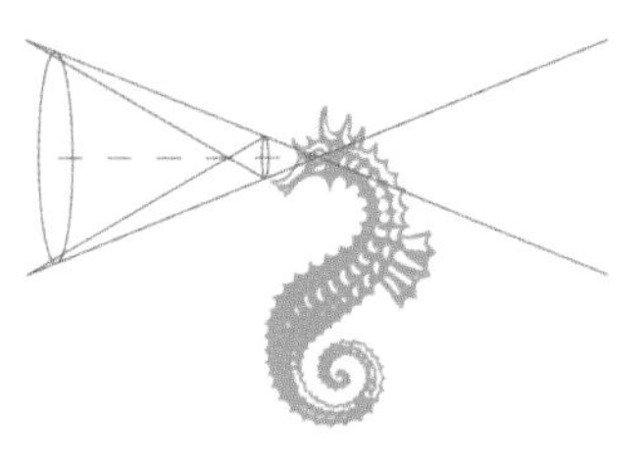

FAR DE TOSSA

FARS DE
LA MEDITERRANIA

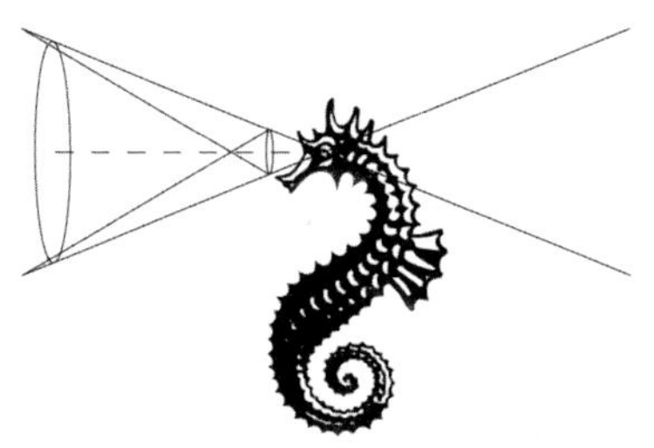

FARS DE
LA MEDITERRANIA

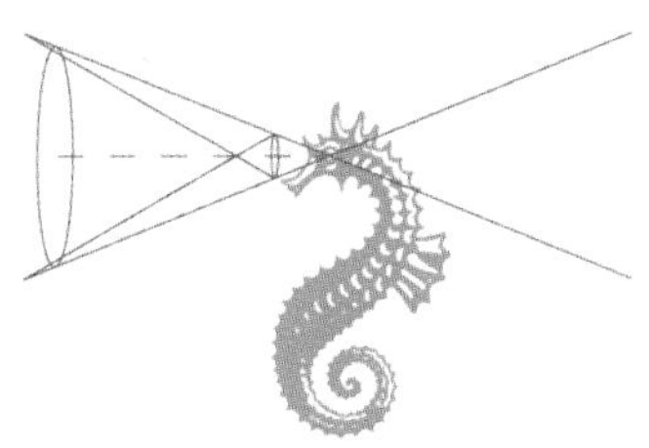

FAR DE TOSSA

CENTRE D'INTERPRETACIÓ DELS FARS DE LA MEDITERRÀNIA

Laken

Client: Laken
Studio: Mister Onüff
Designer: José María Parra
Madrid, Spain
www.misteronuff.com

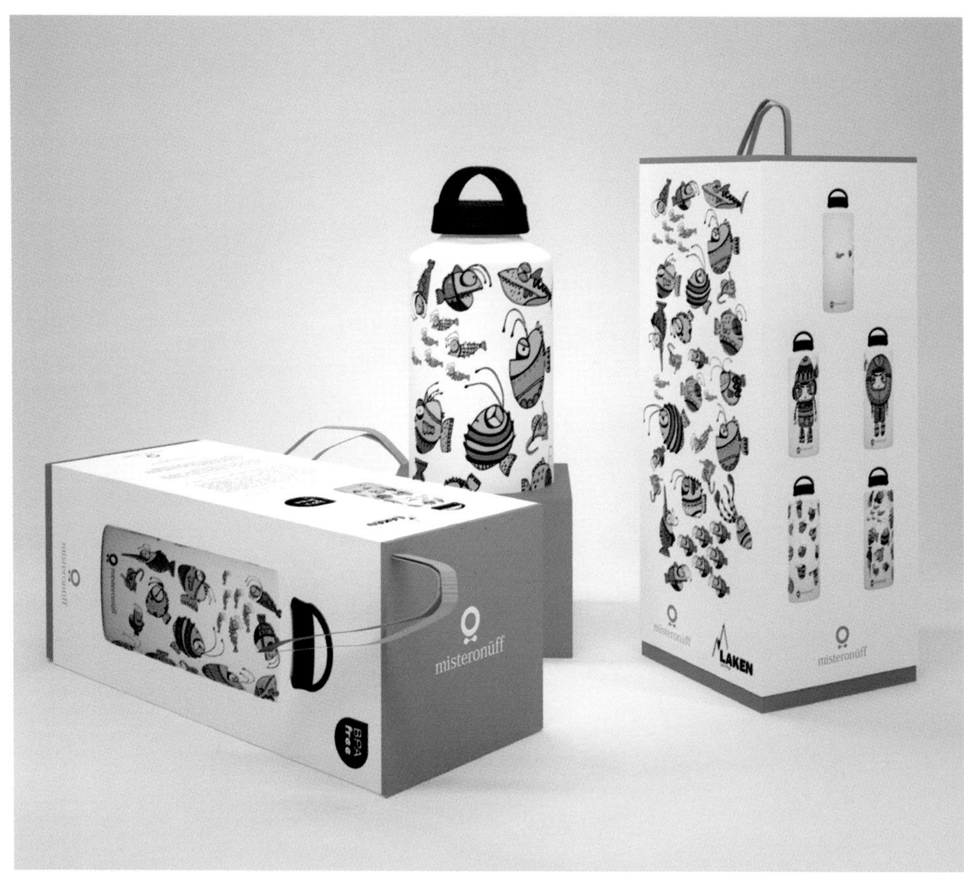

"saw"
misteronüff
misteronüff
misteronüff
misteronüff
"elfo"
"free"
LAKEN

Laken

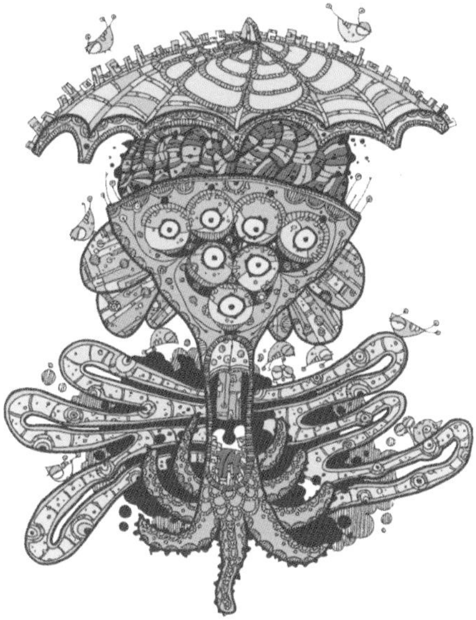

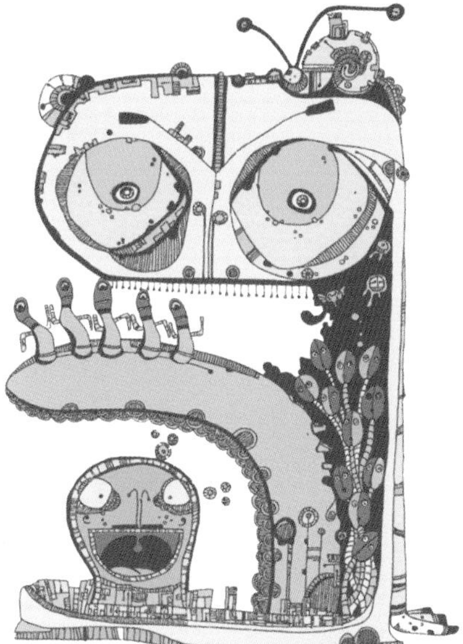

BPA
free
"brain"
LAKEN

BPA
free
"saw"
LAKEN

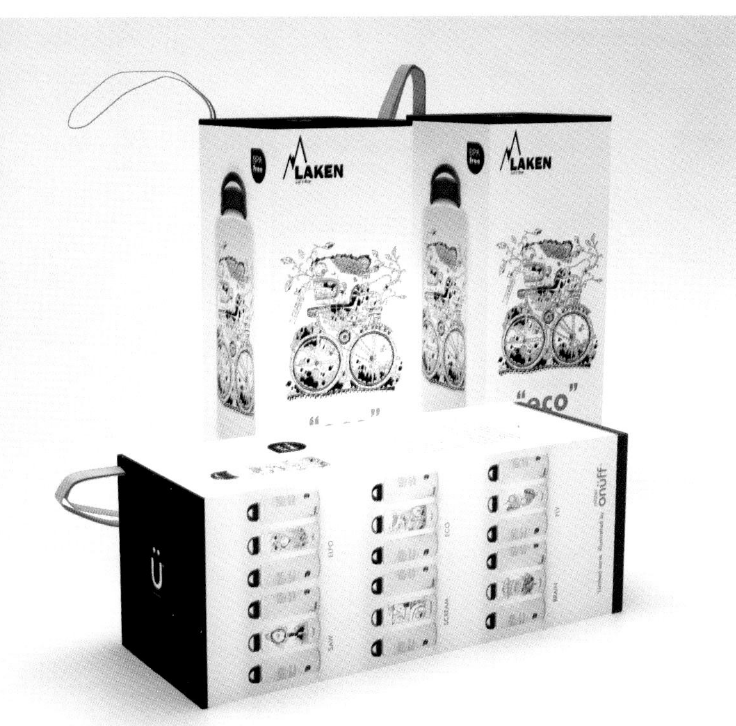
LAKEN
LAKEN
"eco"
ELFO
ECO
FLY
SAW
SCREAM
BRAIN
onüff

LAKEN
"eco"
LAKEN

LAKEN
LAKEN
onüff

Green

Client: Polytrade Paper Corporation Limited
Designer: Eric Chan
Hong Kong, China
www.ericchandesign.com

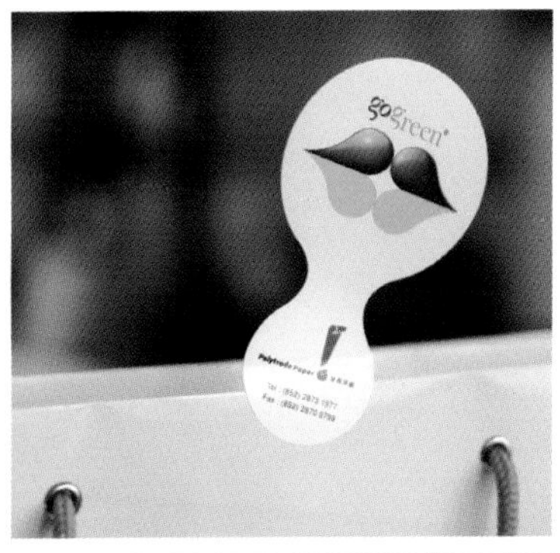
gogreen®
Polytrade Paper

gogreen®
Polytrade Paper
YOUR PERFECT CHOICE

love green®

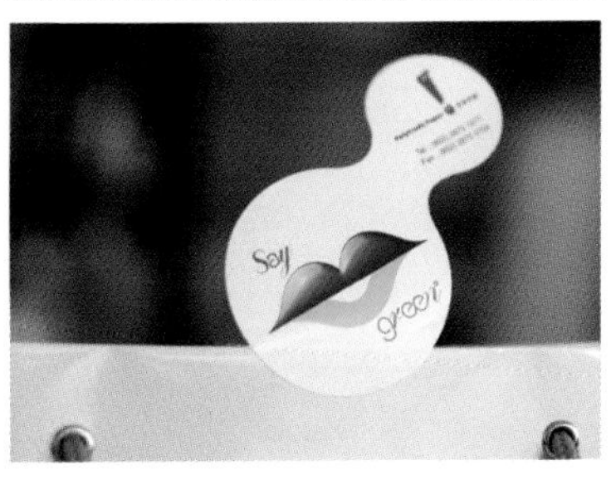
Say
green

love green®

ove green®

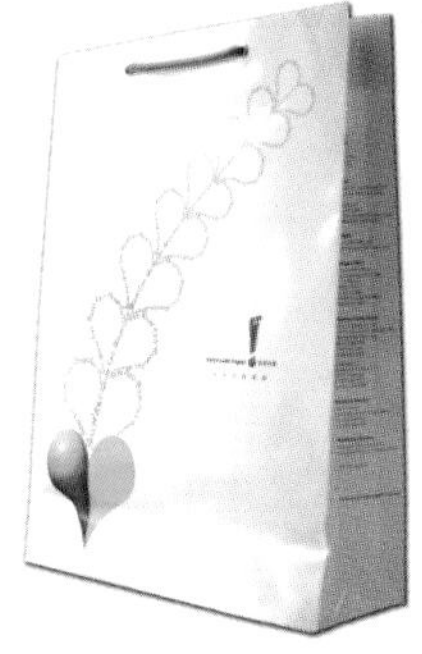

Say
green

Kaori

Client: Floristería Kaori
Designer: Sergio Rey, María Ballesta
Navarra, Spain
sergioreyazcona@gmail.com
m.ballesta@hotmail.com

FLORISTERIA KAORI

KAORI

DISEÑO FLORAL

KAORI

DISEÑO | FLORAL

Kaori

DISEÑO FLORAL

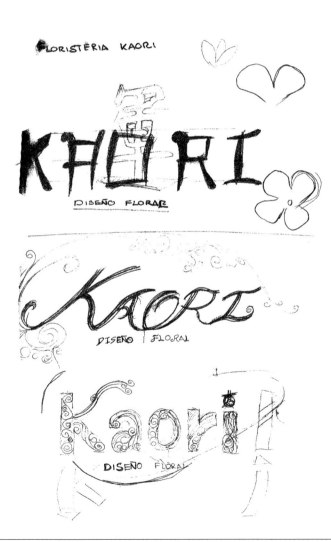

Marc Jacobs

Client: Marc Jacobs / Vogue
Designer: Leandro Dário
São Paulo, Brazil
www.leandrodario.com

Cuines Santa Caterina

Client: Grupo Tragaluz
Designer: Mario Eskenazi
Barcelona, Spain
www.m-eskenazi.com

Santa Caterina Cuines
Cuines Santa Caterina

Santa Caterina Cuines

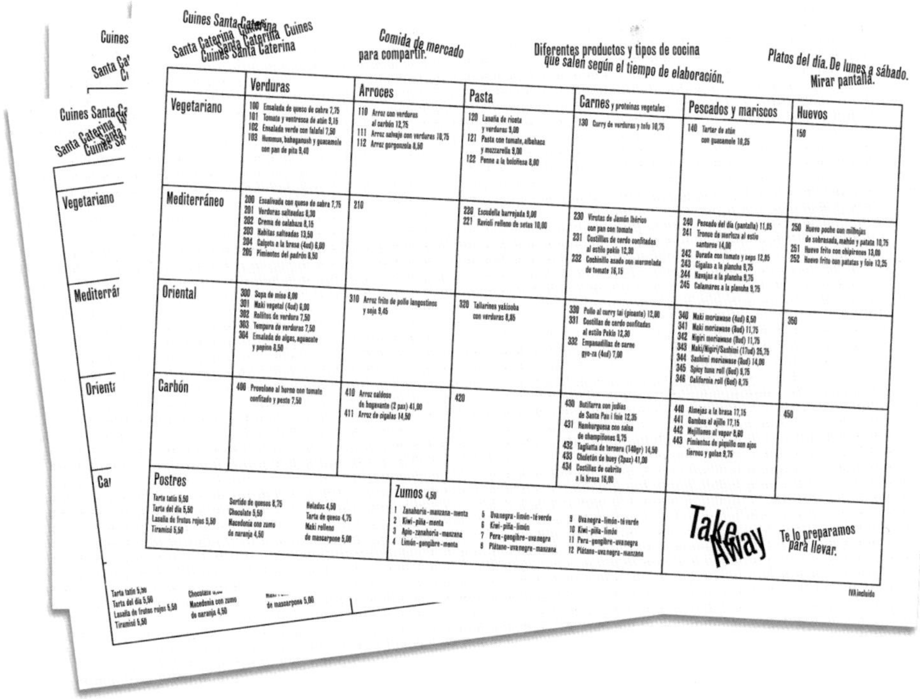

Cuines Santa Caterina

Comida de mercado para compartir.

Diferentes productos y tipos de cocina que salen según el tiempo de elaboración.

Platos del día. De lunes a sábado. Mirar pantalla.

	Verduras	Arroces	Pasta	Carnes y proteínas vegetales	Pescados y mariscos	Huevos
Vegetariano	100 Ensalada de queso de cabra 7,75 101 Tomate y ventresca de atún 9,15 102 Ensalada verde con falafel 7,50 103 Hummus, babaganush y guacamole con pan de pita 9,40	110 Arroz con verduras al carbón 12,75 111 Arroz salvaje con verduras 10,75 112 Arroz gorgonzola 8,50	120 Lasaña de ricota y verduras 9,00 121 Pasta con tomate, albahaca y mozzarella 9,00 122 Penne a la boloñesa 8,00	130 Curry de verduras y tofu 10,75	140 Tartar de atún con guacamole 10,25	150
Mediterráneo	200 Escalivada con queso de sabra 7,75 201 Verduras salteadas 8,30 202 Crema de calabaza 8,15 203 Habitas salteadas 13,50 204 Calçots a la brasa (4ud) 6,00 205 Pimientos del padrón 8,50	210	220 Escudella barrejada 9,00 221 Ravioli relleno de setas 10,00	230 Virutas de Jamón Ibérico con pan con tomate 231 Costillas de cerdo confitadas al estilo pekín 12,30 232 Cochinillo asado con mermelada de tomate 16,15	240 Pescado del día (pantalla) 11,85 241 Tronco de merluza al estilo santurce 14,00 242 Dorada con tomate y ceps 12,85 243 Cigalas a la plancha 9,75 244 Navajas a la plancha 9,75 245 Calamares a la plancha 9,75	250 Huevo poche con milhojas de sobrasada, mahón y patata 10,75 251 Huevo frito con chipirones 13,00 252 Huevo frito con patatas y foie 13,25
Oriental	300 Sopa de miso 8,00 301 Maki vegetal (4ud) 6,00 302 Rollitos de verdura 7,50 303 Tempura de verduras 7,50 304 Ensalada de algas, aguacate y pepino 8,50	310 Arroz frito de pollo langostinos y soja 9,45	320 Tallarines yakisoba con verduras 8,85	330 Pollo al curry tai (picante) 12,00 331 Costillas de cerdo confitadas al estilo Pekín 12,30 332 Empanadillas de carne gyo-za (4ud) 7,00	340 Maki moriawase (4ud) 6,50 341 Maki moriawase (8ud) 11,75 342 Nigiri moriawase (8ud) 11,75 343 Maki/Nigiri/Sashimi (17ud) 25,75 344 Sashimi moriawase (8ud) 14,00 345 Spicy tuna roll (6ud) 9,75 346 California roll (6ud) 8,75	350
Carbón	400 Provolone al horno con tomate confitado y pesto 7,50	410 Arroz caldoso de bogavante (2 pax) 41,00 411 Arroz de cigalas 14,50	420	430 Butifarra con judías de Santa Pau i foie 12,35 431 Hamburguesa con salsa de champiñones 9,75 432 Tagliatta de ternera (140gr) 14,50 433 Chuletón de buey (2pax) 41,00 434 Costillas de cabrito a la brasa 16,00	440 Almejas a la brasa 17,15 441 Gambas al ajillo 17,15 442 Mejillones al vapor 8,60 443 Pimientos de piquillo con ajos tiernos y gulas 9,75	450

Postres

Tarta tatín 5,50
Tarta del día 5,50
Lasaña de frutos rojos 5,50
Tiramisú 5,50
Surtido de quesos 8,75
Chocolate 5,50
Macedonia con zumo de naranja 4,50
Helados 4,50
Tarta de queso 4,75
Maki relleno de mascarpone 5,00

Zumos 4,50

1 Zanahoria-manzana-menta
2 Kiwi-piña-menta
3 Apio-zanahoria-manzana
4 Limón-gengibre-menta
5 Uva negra-limón-té verde
6 Kiwi-piña-limón
7 Pera-gengibre-uva negra
8 Plátano-uva negra-manzana
9 Uva negra-limón-té verde
10 Kiwi-piña-limón
11 Pera-gengibre-uva negra
12 Plátano-uva negra-manzana

Take Away
Te lo preparamos para llevar.

IVA incluido

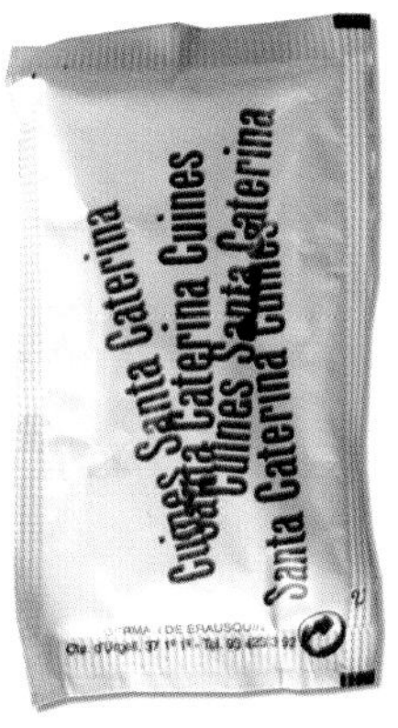

Cuines Santa Caterina
Santa Caterina Cuines
Santa Caterina Cuines

Santa Caterina Cuines
Santa Caterina Cuines
Cuines Santa Caterina

parada tapes, entrepans i sucs
parada amanides i verdures
parada mediterrània
parada asiàtica
parada pastes i rissotos

Mercat Santa Caterina
(al costat de la Catedral)
T 932 689 918
www.cuinessantacaterina.com

GRUPO TRAGALUZ

DEL MORDISCO

Cuines Santa Caterina

Social Urban

Client: Social Urban
Designer: Xosé Teiga
Santiago de Compostela, Spain
www.xoseteiga.com

Luxury Spain

Client: Asociación Española de Lujo
Studio: Inercia grafica
Designer: Alex Moreno
Castelldefels, Spain
www.inerciagrafica.com

LUXURY SPAIN
Asociación Española de Lujo

LUXURY SPAIN
Asociación Española de Lujo
COCKTAIL PARTY en Bankers Bar
Hotel Mandarin Oriental Barcelona
Con sorteo exclusivo
THE SHOPPING NIGHT BARCELONA
2 de Diciembre 2010
Inicio sorteo privado
a la 1h. a.m.
www.luxuryspain.es
Participan en el sorteo
ASTON MARTIN
Barcelona
santa eulalia
Barcelona 1843
GODIVA
Belgium 1926
CAVIAR HOUSE & PRUNIER
TCN
Blai Limousines
luxury car rental
Colaboran
BANKERS BAR
MANDARIN ORIENTAL
BARCELONA
TOTÉ VIGNAU
inercia
n° sorteo: 0010
Nombre:
Apellidos:
Teléfono:
Mail:
Población:

Luxury Spain

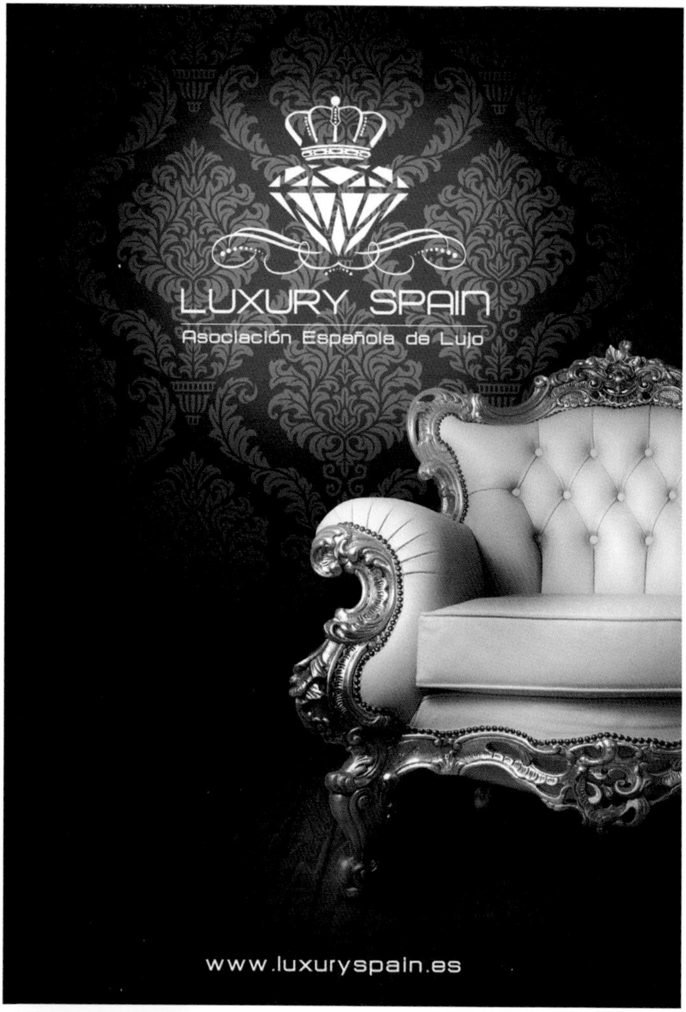

LUXURY SPAIN
Asociación Española de Lujo
www.luxuryspain.es

LUXURY SPAIN
Asociación Española de Lujo
www.luxuryspain.es

LUXURY SPAIN
Asociación Española de Lujo
Cristina Martin Blasi
GENERAL MANAGER
+34 620 68 19 40
Paseo de Gracia 118, principal - 08008 Barcelona
T. 93 244 44 95 - direccion@luxuryspain.es
www.luxuryspain.es

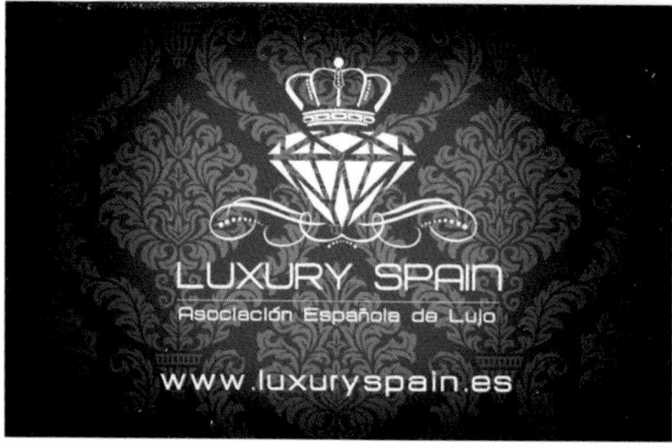

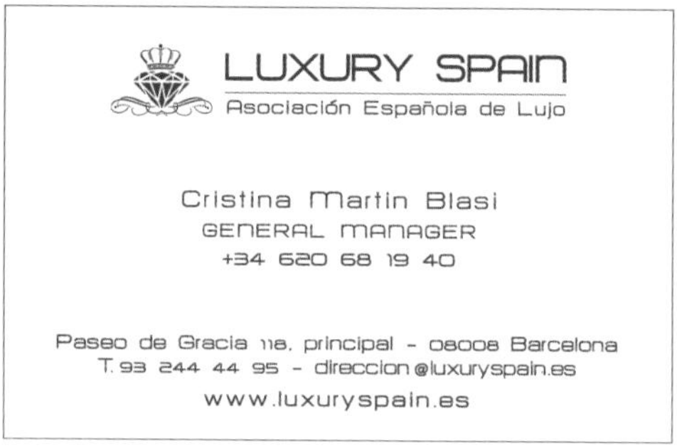

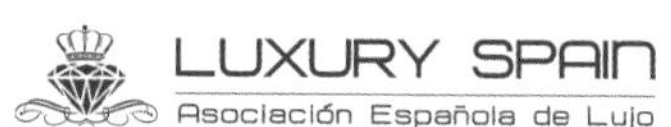

Margarida Llabrés

Client: Margarida Llabrés
Studio: Dúctil
Designer: Damià Rotger Miró
Mallorca, Spain
www.ductilct.com

Hazel

Client: Hazel. Guillermo Padellano
Designer: Marina Company
Barcelona, Spain
www.mirindacompany.com

HAZEL

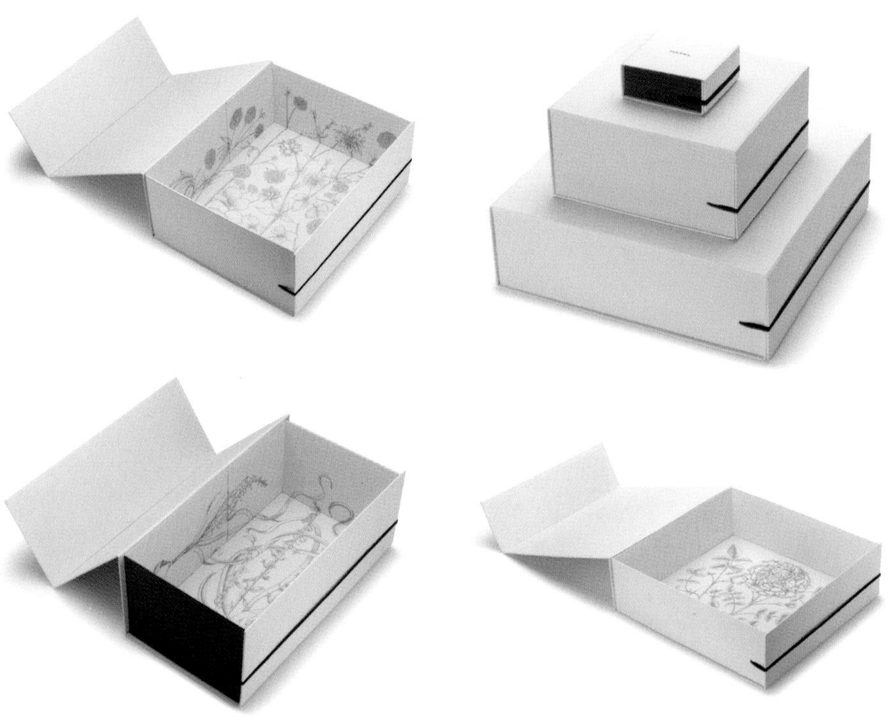

HAZEL
HAZEL
HAZEL
flos constantinopolitanus
tulipa polyanthos praeox
hyacinthus serotinus
www.hazel.es
www.hazel.es
www.hazel.es

Hazel

López Santos 4, planta 1°
28230 Las Rozas, Madrid
Tel. +34 91 616 97 65
Fax +34 91 616 97 66

Hazel

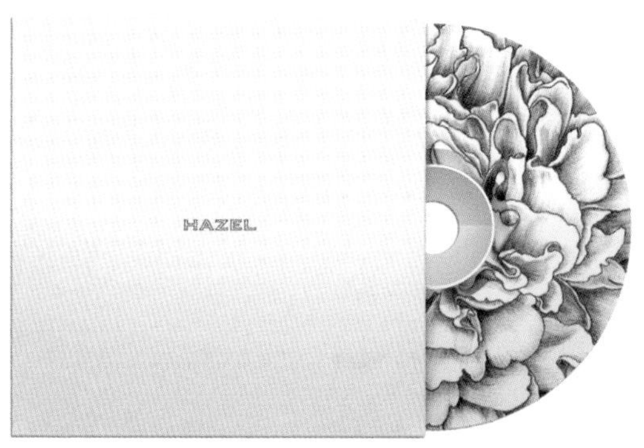

HAZEL

Guillermo Padellano
director general

gpadellano@hazel.es

López Santos 4, planta 1ª
28230 Las Rozas, Madrid.
Tel. +34 91 616 97 65
Fax +34 91 616 97 66

Soledad Calvo
directora de compras

soledad.calvo@hazel.es

López Santos 4, planta 1ª
28230 Las Rozas, Madrid.
Tel. +34 91 616 97 65
Fax +34 91 616 97 66

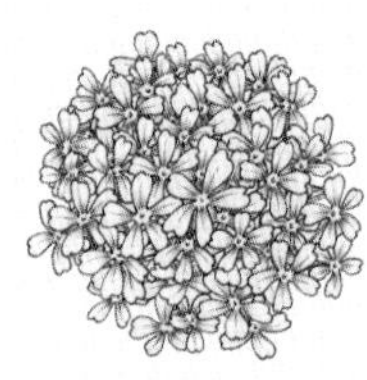

Teresa Polo
responsable RRHH

teresa.polo@hazel.es

López Santos 4, planta 1ª
28230 Las Rozas, Madrid.
Tel. +34 91 616 97 65
Fax +34 91 616 97 66

Tomás Romero
director de tiendas

tomas.romero@hazel.es
mobil 618756069

López Santos 4, planta 1ª
28230 Las Rozas, Madrid.
Tel. +34 91 616 97 65
Fax +34 91 616 97 66

Delphine Costenoble
merchandising visual

delphine.costenoble@hazel.es

López Santos 4, planta 1ª
28230 Las Rozas, Madrid.
Tel. +34 91 616 97 65
Fax +34 91 616 97 66

ZìZài Dermatology

Client: ZìZài Dermatology
Studio: Tenfold Collective
Lovcland, CO, USA
www.tenfoldcollective.com

Adidas T-Boy

Client: Adidas
Designer: Shin Tanaka
Portland, Oregon, USA
www.shin.co.nr

adidas

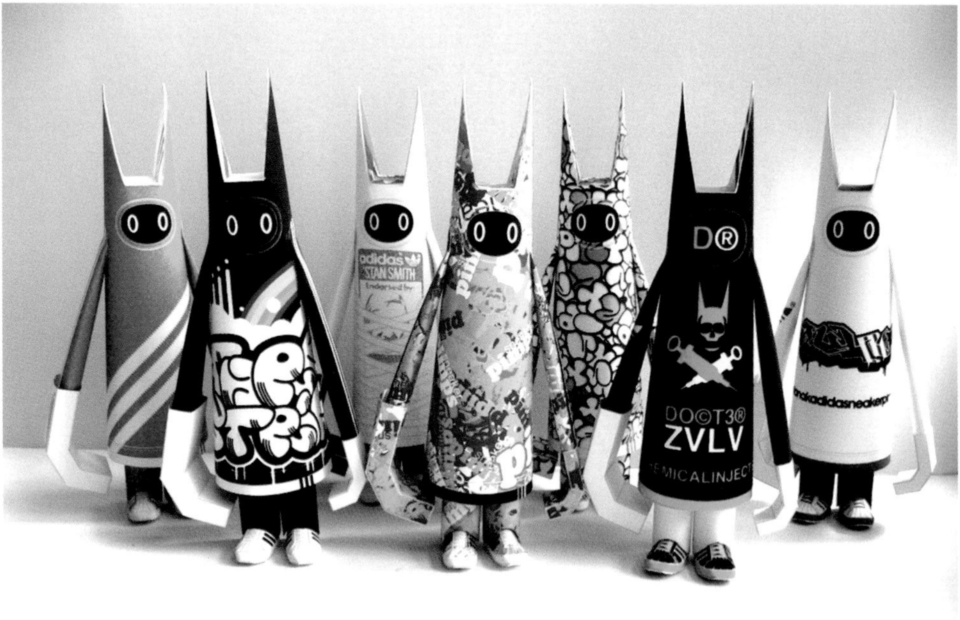
adidas
STAN SMITH
Endorsed by
D®
DO©T3®
ZVLV
EMICALINJECT

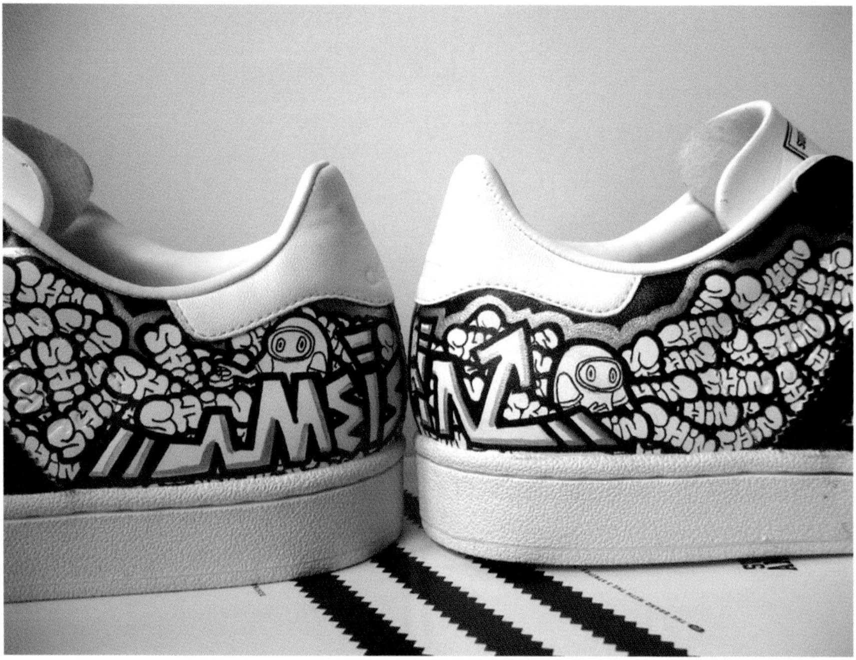

ADIDAS X T-BOY

T-BOY IS AN COLLECTABLE HANDMADED PAPER FIGURE
INSPIRED FROM CHILDREN PULLING THEIR TEES OVER THEIR HEAD

T-BOY SHOW

by SHIN TANAKA

February
2006

Just Be Complex/
Compound Gallery
Portland
Oregon
US

adidas

T-BOY
PAPER 100%
COMPOUND
GALLERY

http://shin.co.nr/
http://www.adidas.com/
http://www.justbedesign.com/

Adidas T-Boy

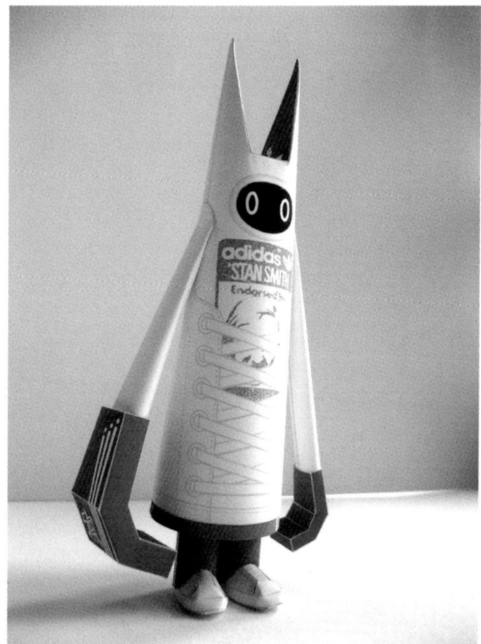
adidas
STAN SMITH
Endorsed by

Kindergarden Izvor

Client: Kindergarden Izvor-Samobor
Studio: Studio Snooze
Designer: Studio Snooze
Samobor, Croatian
www.studiosnooze.com

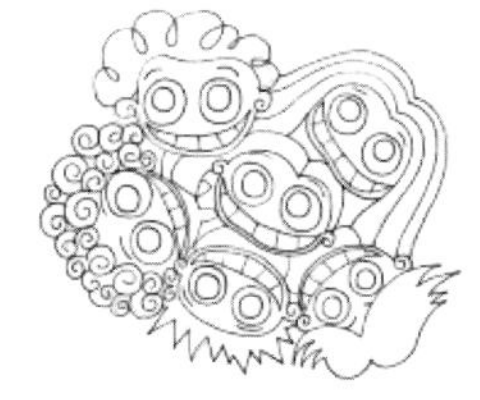

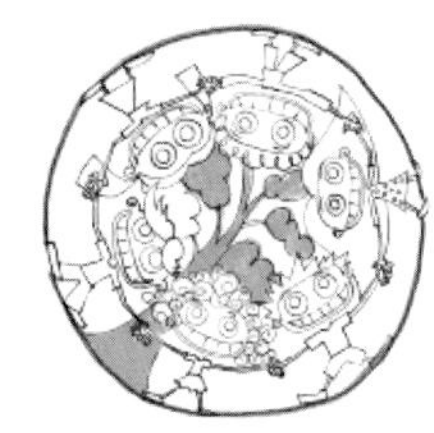

dječji vrtić
IZVOR
samobor

DJEČJI VRTIĆ
IZVOR

Ljerka Cigula
ravnateljica
dječji vrtić
IZVOR
samobor

Igor Kuhar
psiholog
dječji vrtić
IZVOR
samobor

DJEČJI VRTIĆ IZVOR

BrandScents

Client: Turnstyle (Self-Promotion)
Studio: Turnstyle
Creative Director: Steve Watson
Designer: Steve Watson
Seattle, USA
www.turnstylestudio.com

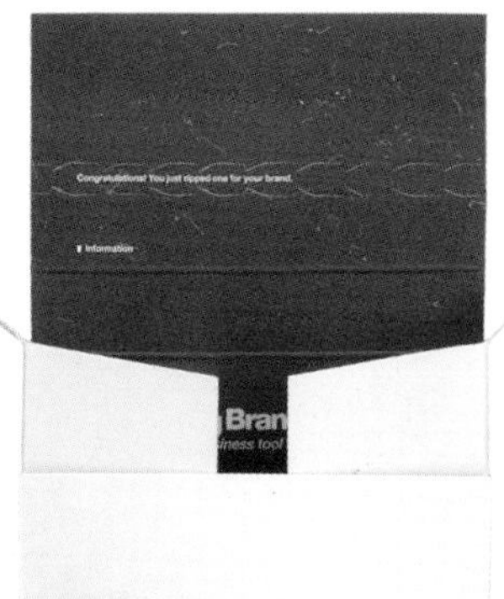

BrandScents™
Be Different. Smell Different.

sealed for freshness
Does your brand stink?

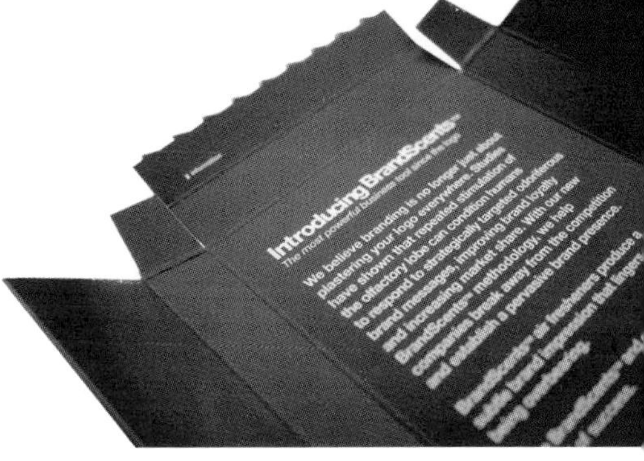
Introducing BrandScents™
The most powerful business tool since the logo
We believe branding is no longer just about plastering your logo everywhere. Studies have shown that repeated stimulation of the olfactory lobe can condition humans to respond to strategically targeted odoriferous brand messages, improving brand loyalty and increasing market share. With our new BrandScents™ methodology, we help companies break away from the competition and establish a pervasive brand presence.

turnstyle
BrandScents™
Be Different. Smell Different.
6

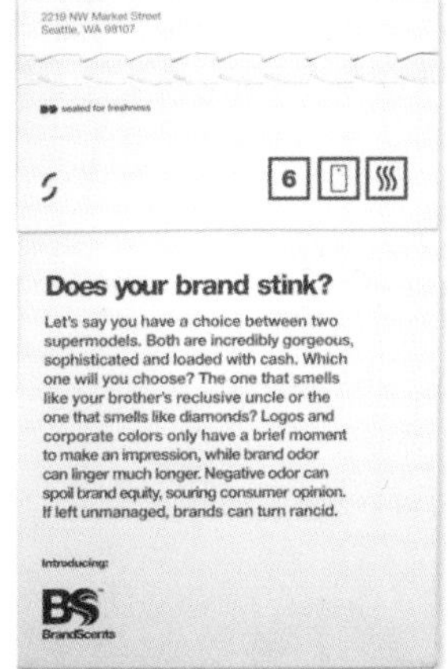
2219 NW Market Street
Seattle, WA 98107
sealed for freshness
6
Does your brand stink?
Let's say you have a choice between two supermodels. Both are incredibly gorgeous, sophisticated and loaded with cash. Which one will you choose? The one that smells like your brother's reclusive uncle or the one that smells like diamonds? Logos and corporate colors only have a brief moment to make an impression, while brand odor can linger much longer. Negative odor can spoil brand equity, souring consumer opinion. If left unmanaged, brands can turn rancid.
Introducing:
BS
BrandScents

BS™
BrandScents
Innovation
Anyone who thinks the sky is the limit has not seen Star Wars.
turnstyle

BS™
BrandScents
Scent No. | 002
Formulation Date: 12/07
Category: Brand Values
Prepared By: Turnstyle
Integrity
In matters of principle, stand like a rock. Or a statue.
turnstyle

South Am. Roads

Client: South America Roads
Studio: Rgb/Dg
Designer: Rodrigo Broner
Buenos Aires, Argentina
www.rgbdg.com.ar

SOUTH
AMERICAN
ROADS

SOUTH
AMERICAN
ROADS
Live unique experiences driving 4x4 vehicles
skip
EMPIRE OF
BRAZIL
PERU
BOLIVIA
OCEAN
Peace
Nature

TRACK 1 | TRACK 2 | TRACK 3 | OFF
ENGLISH | SPANISH
SOUTH
AMERICAN
ROADS
Experiences
About Us
Experiences
Vehicles
Gallery
Contact
"Argentina is an ideal country for the independent traveler that wants to explore different lands and cultures without the pression of time, letting themselves be led on their senses and emotions. Meet our native people and experience their hospitality, visit small villages lost in time and wonderful and virgin landscapes where the man has not transformed the purity of the air, the brightness of the sky and the deep strerry nights.
Let yourself the chance to live a unique and gratifying experience!"
SOUTH AMERICAN WINES & FLAVORS
SOUTH AMERICAN ADVENTURE
SOUTH AMERICAN DISCOVERY
Unique landscapes and cultures show its colorful dishes and exquisite flavors. Taste and learn how to prepare our typical "empanada" and the traditional argentinean "asado". The Wines
Driving an excellent 4x4 truck, an incredible combination between outdoor activities and unique landscapes will be at your disposal. Horseback ridings along vineyards, hikings
The impressive altitude of the Andes and the immensity of Salta Salt lakes as well as the rich culture of the Argentinean Northwest and the signs of prehistoric life in Talampaya and

Pretty Green

Client: PrettyGreen
Studio: Design Friendship
London, United Kingdom
www.designfriendship.com

PrettyGreen

www.theprettygreen.com

Ariadne Muñoz

Client: Ariadne Muñoz
Studio: Limón Studio
Designer: Claudio Limón
Jalisco, Mexico
www.cargocollective.com/limonestudio

ENCUENTRA
tu razón para ser feliz
PIENSA
primero en ti
BUSCA
el poder de tus pensamientos
CAMBIA
tu forma de ver la vida
ARIADNE MUÑOZ
psicóloga

Getxophoto

Client: Getxophoto
Studio: Barfutura
Madrid, Spain
www.barfutura.com

yel Trillo 10

TICAS JUVENILES. TRES DÉCADAS

de la Frontera, 1953. Hiri handien kaleak
gokoena bezala hartu ditu eta horietan
orronteak erretratatu ditu azken 30
. Bere lanak rock, pop edota rap-aren
rputza identitate zeinu eta leku batzuk
rako gune bihurtu dituen internazional
akusten du.

la Frontera, 1953. Ha hecho de las calles de
s ciudades su plató favorito, en el que ha ido
las corrientes musicales a lo largo de estos
años. Su fotografía refleja una internacional
a través del rock, del pop, del rap, ha
el cuerpo en un signo de identidad y ciertos
n territorios creativos.

Osama Esid

JUEGO DE REPRESENTACIONES;
EL EXPERIMENTO EGIPCIO

Damasko, 1970. Mendebaldean eta ekialdean
iraganean sortutako eta moduren batean inkon
kolektiboan bizirik dauden gizarte ikuskerak et
estereotipoak aztertu ditu. Ekialdetasuna, bere
konnotazio exotiko eta sentsualekin aztertzea
topikoak sortzeko mekanismoetan dauden
kontraesanak agerian jartzen dituen aukera so
eta teorikoak sortu ditu.

Damasco, 1970. Su trabajo investiga las visio
y estereotipos sociales que desde occidente y
oriente se han creado en el pasado, y que pe
en el inconsciente colectivo. Su indagación so
el orientalismo, con sus connotaciones exótic
sensuales, genera un abanico de posibilidade
y teóricas que pone de manifiesto las contra
existentes en los mecanismos de creación d

Babesle berezia / Patrocinio especial: Eusko Jaurlar
Zuzendaritza / Dirección de Inmigración del Gobierno

13

Kwame Apagya

PORTRAITS

. Erretratatuei jeneralean ezin lor
gloria momentu batean edukitzeko
en die: telebistak barra armairuetan,
erno ondo hornituak... dibertigarriak izan
pologiak, baina nahigabe kezkagarriak
ere, mendabalderako joera eta amets

Photomuseum Argazki & Zinema Museoa

XX. MENDEKO ARGAZKIGINTZA KATALANA

Zarauzko Photomuseum Argazki & Zinema Museoak
XX mendeko argazki gintza katalana. Hurbilketa bat
aurkezten du, 30 irudi eta 14 egileren aukeraketa,
denak Reus hiriari lotuak, argazkigintzaren artean

FOTOGRAFÍA CATALANA DEL SIG

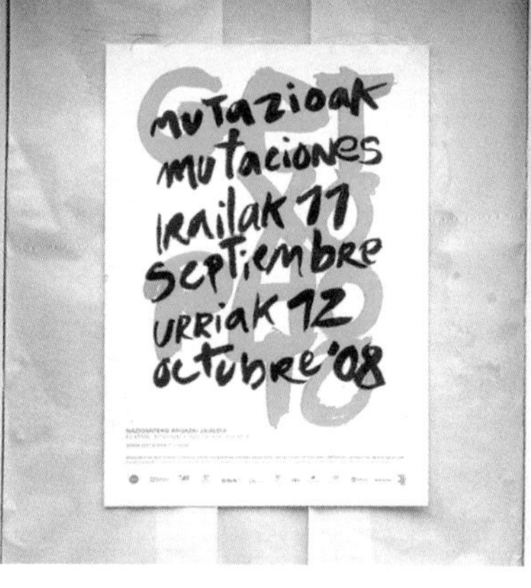

Getxophoto

mutazioak
mutaciones
irailak 11
septiembre
urriak 12
octubre '08
NAZIOARTEKO ARGAZKI JAIALDIA
FESTIVAL INTERNACIONAL DE FOTOGRAFÍA

GET
XO
PHO
TO
Philip Kwame
Apagya
STUDIO PORTRAITS

Esteban Pastorino NANJING
GET
XO
PHO
TO

Pere Formiguera

Miguel Trillo

GET
XO
PHO
TO

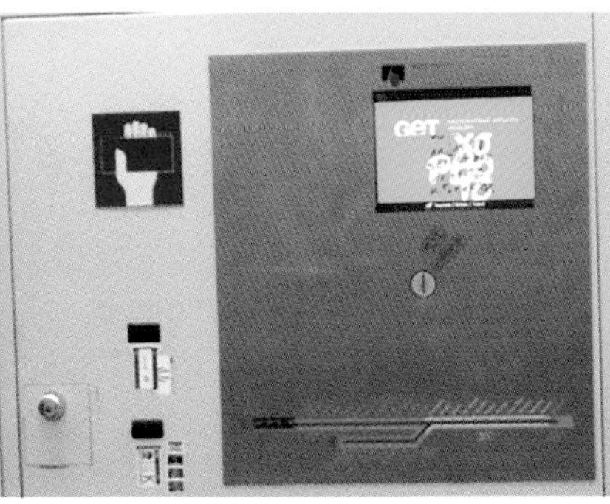

The black shooter

Client: Santi Rodríguez
Studio: Xosé Teiga
Designer: Xosé Teiga
Santiago de Compostela, Spain
www.xoseteiga.com

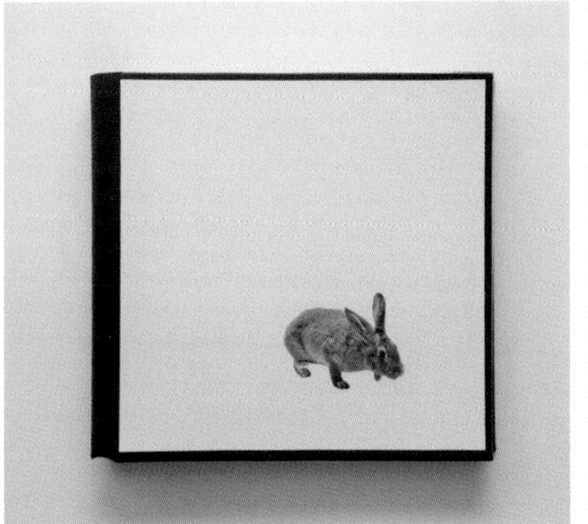

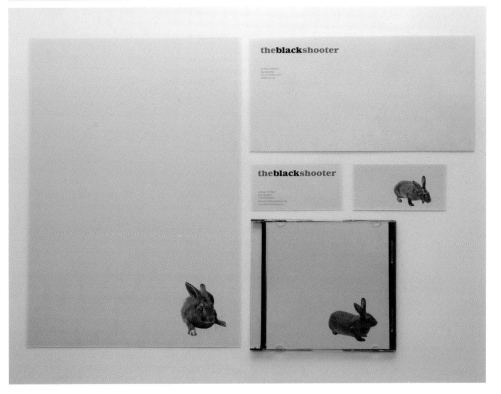
theblackshooter
santiago rodriguez
photographer

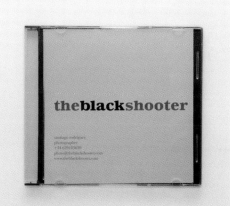

Cavalló Graula

Client: Cava Cavalló Graula
Studio: Inercia gráfica
Designer: Alex Moreno
Castelldefels, Spain
www.inerciagrafica.com

CAVALLÓ GRAULA

CAVALLÓ GRAULA

www.cavallograula.com

Cavalló Graula

CG
CAVALLÓ GRAULA
CAVA
CAVA
Brut nature
CG
CAVALLÓ GRAULA
CAVA
CAVA
CAVA
CAVA
CG
CAVALLÓ GRAULA
CAVA
CAVA
CG
CAVALLÓ GRAULA
CAVA BRUT
CAVA BRUT
Rosado
Rosado

Sans & Sans

Client: Sans&Sans. Fine Tea merchants
Designer: Sonsoles Llorens
Barcelona, Spain
www.sonsoles.com

SANS & SANS
FINE TEA MERCHANTS

SANS & SANS
FINE TEA MERCHANTS

Sans & Sans

SANS & SANS
FANTASIA COLLECTION
Mil y Una Noches
PEACH, APRICOT AND NECTARINE

SANS & SANS
FINE TEA MERCHANTS

SANS & SANS
FINE TEA MERCHANTS

SANS & SANS

The Apartment

Client: The Apartment
Studio: The Luxury of Protest
Creative director and copywriter: Stefan Boublil
Designer and illustrator: Peter Crnokrak
London, United Kingdom
www.theluxuryofprotest.com

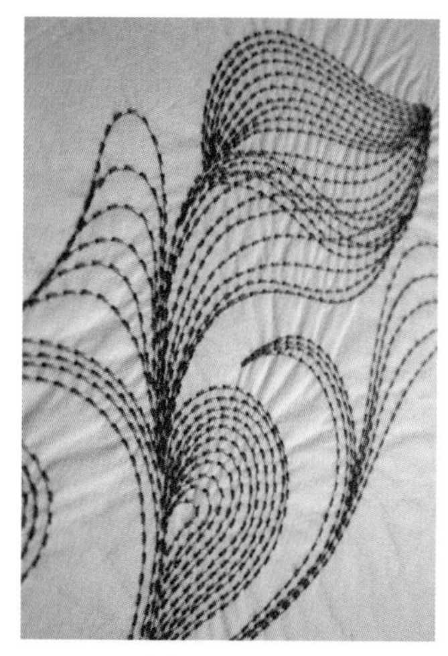

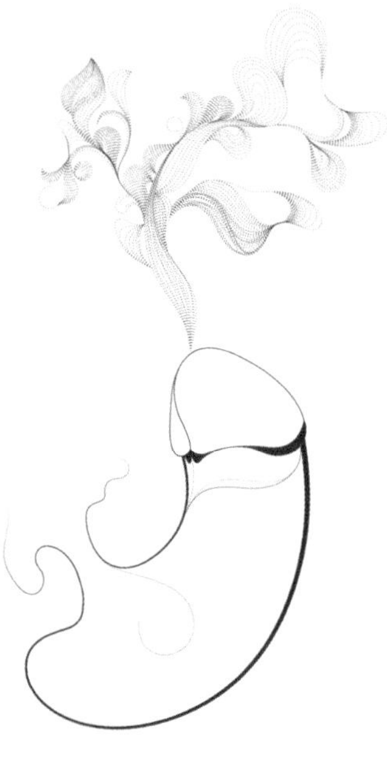

the
apartment.
& ADDRESS:
101 Crosby
Street
NY, NY 10012
U.S.A.
theapt.com

the
apartment.
& JESUS &
TALENT & ART
& HONG KONG
& OPINION &
MUSIC &
NSFW & CO-
PENHAGEN &
TOKYO &
MILAN &
WEB &
MONTRÉAL
& FASHION &
NEWS & TV &
PARIS &
BOOKS & AR-
CHITECTURE
& SUCKS &
DESIGN & RIO
DE JANEIRO &
LONDON
& SHANGHAI
& MOVIES &
MARKETING
& GEAR
REPORT &
STOCKHOLM
& AWESOME
& ISTANBUL &
GOT A MINUTE
& ADDRESS:
101 Crosby
Street
NEW YORK
10012
WEBSITE:
theapt.com
P.212.219.3661
F.212.219.3683

the
apartment.
& ADDRESS:
101 Crosby
Street
NY, NY 10012
U.S.A.
theapt.com
P.212.219.3661

___REQUEST
___NEWS
___REVIEW
___THANK YOU
___REGARDS
___INVITATION

the
apartment.
& NSFW &
BARCELONA &
ART &
MONTRÉAL &
FASHION &
SUCKS & WEB
& TOKYO

101 Crosby
Street
NYC 10012
__________@
theapt.com
P.212.219.3661
ext.___

Beirut Art Center

Client: Beirut Art Center
Studio: Vit-e Design Studio
Art director: Nathalie Fallaha
Designer: Nathalie Fallaha
Beirut, Liebanon
www.vit-e.com

BEIRUT ART CENTER
مركز بيروت للفن

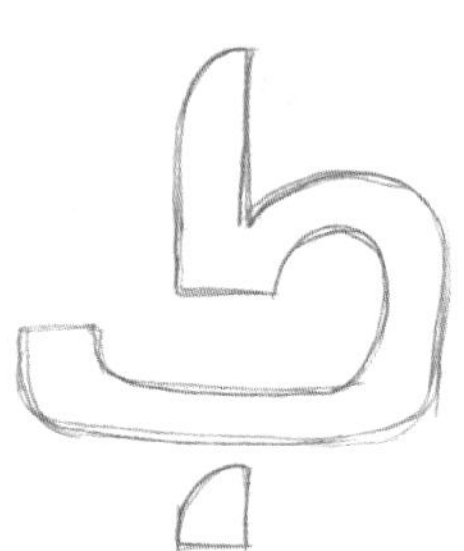

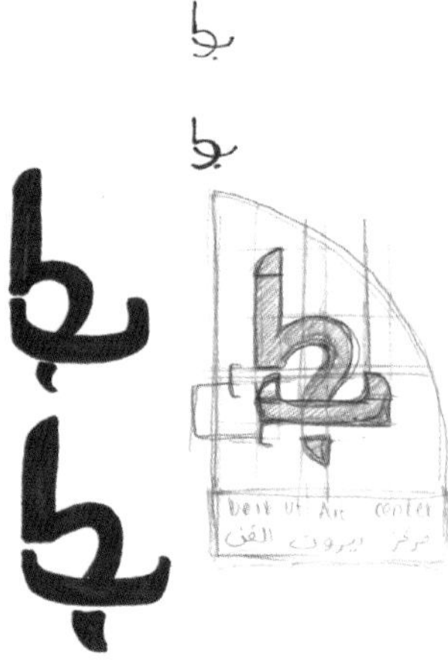

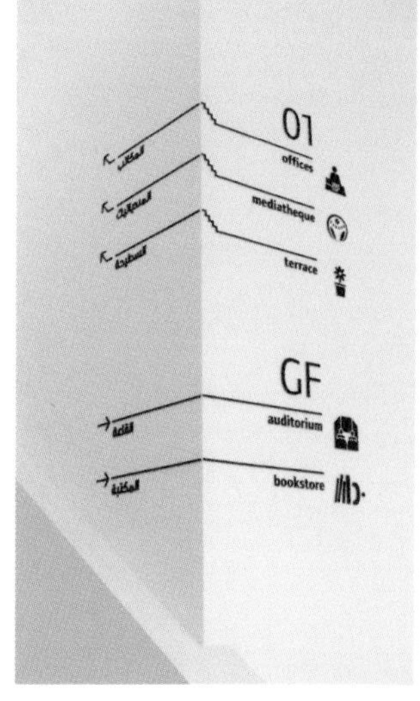

CLOSER
اقتراب
january 16 ● april 2. 2009
١٦ كانون الثاني ● ٢ نيسان ٢٠٠٩
Jananne Al-Ani جنان العاني
Tony Chakar طوني شكر
Antoine D'Agata أنطوان داغاتا
Mona Hatoum منى حاطوم
Emily Jacir إميلي جاسر
Jill Magid جيل ماجيد
Anri Sala أنري سالا
Lina Saneh لينا صانع
Lisa Steele ليزا ستيل
Akram Zaatari اكرم زعتري
Cynthia Zaven سنتيا زافين
BEIRUT ART CENTER
مركز بيروت للفن
Mona Hatoum
منى حاطوم
June 10 ● September 9. 2010
١٠ حزيران ● ٩ أيلول ٢٠١٠
Witness
شاهد
BRITISH COUNCIL
BEIRUT ART CENTER
مركز بيروت للفن
Mona Hatoum
منى حاطوم
Witness
شاهد
CLOSER
EXPOSURE 2009
اقتراب
Akram Zaatari
أكرم زعتري

BEIRUT ART CENTER
مركز بيروت للفن

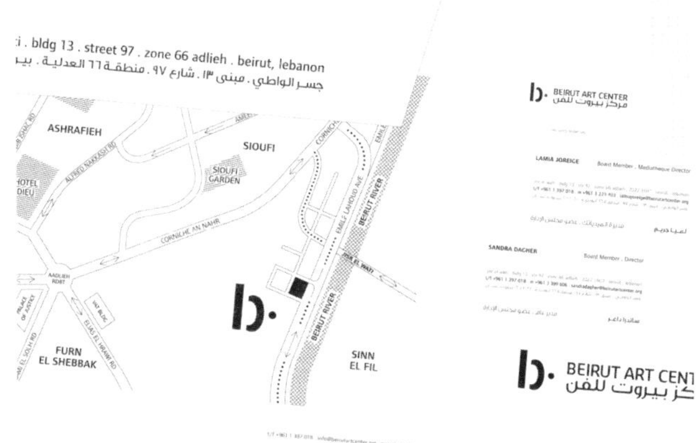
i . bldg 13 . street 97 . zone 66 adlieh . beirut, lebanon
جسر الواطي . مبنى ١٣ . شارع ٩٧ . منطقة ٦٦ العدلية . بير
ASHRAFIEH
SIOUFI
SIOUFI GARDEN
HOTEL DIEU
CORNICHE AN NAHR
BEIRUT RIVER
EMILE LAHOUD AVE
FURN EL SHEBBAK
SINN EL FIL
BEIRUT ART CENTER
مركز بيروت للفن
LAMIA JOREIGE
Board Member . Mediatheque Director
SANDRA DAGHER
Board Member . Director
BEIRUT ART CEN
كز بيروت للفن

Mercado de San Miguel

Client: Mercado de San Miguel
Studio: Carrió Sánchez Lacasta
Creative strategy: Nadie. The creative think tank
Madrid, Spain
www.carriosanchezlacasta.com

Plaza de Oriente, 3 Bajo dcha.
28013 Madrid
t +34 915 424 936
f +34 915 592 744
www.mercadosanmiguel.es

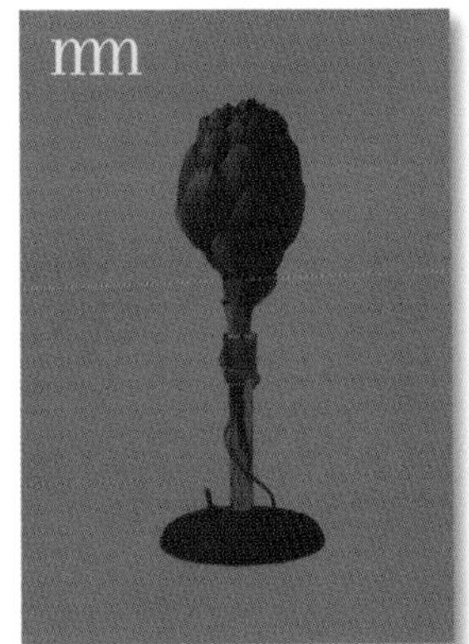

Kapulica

Client: Kapulica Studio
Studio: Buch Design
London/Zagreb, United Kingdom/Croatia
www.bunchdesign.com

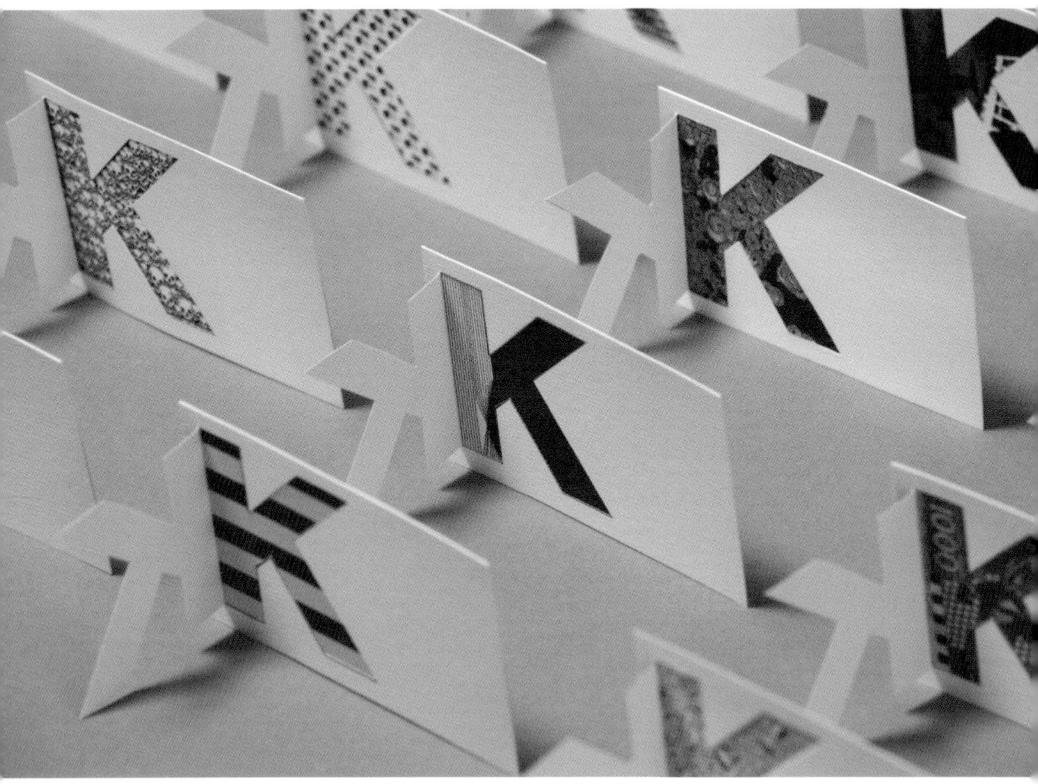

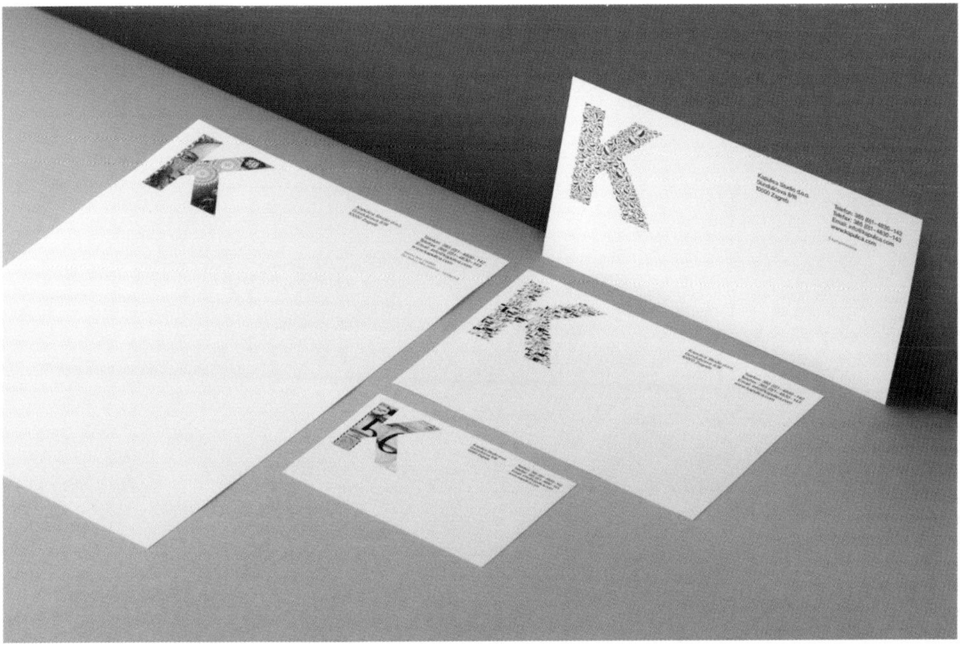

Kapulica

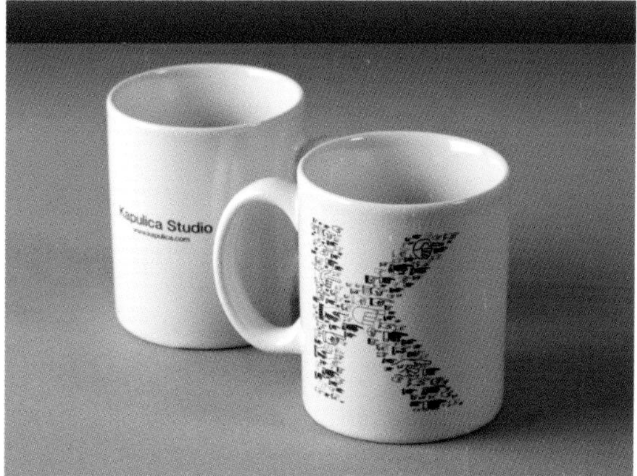
Kapulica Studio

Feeling

Client: Feeling Shop.es
Studio: Inercia gráfica
Designer: Alex Moreno
Castelldefels, Spain
www.inerciagrafica.com

Feeling
shop

FEELING
shop

Feeling
shop

Feeling

PRODUCTOS ERÓTICOS I LENCERIA FINA I REUNIONES TUPPERSEX I GABINETE SEXOLÓGICO

www.feelingshop.es

Feelingshop

Feelingshop

iDEOlab

Client: iDEOlab
Studio: iDEOlab
Vitoria-Gasteiz, Spain
www.ideolab.com

GRAPHIC
DESIGN
web

IDEOlab
Viena 16, bajo izqda.
01002 Vitoria-Gasteiz
Tel.: 945 258 196
info@ideolab.com

IDEOlab

Hotel Omm

Client: Grupo Tragaluz
Designer: Mario Eskenazi
Barcelona, Spain
www.m-eskenazi.com

Hotel Omm

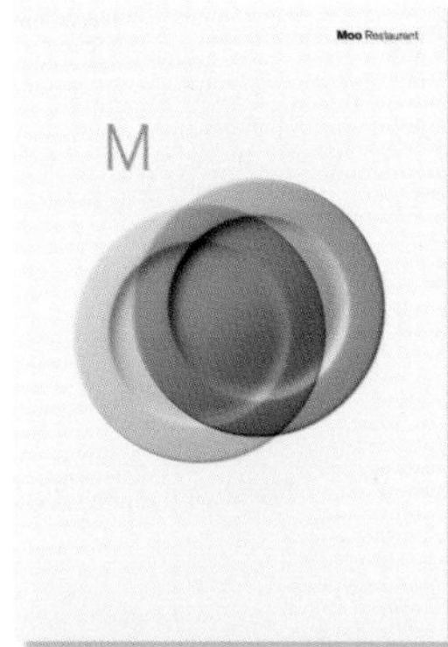
Moo Restaurant
M

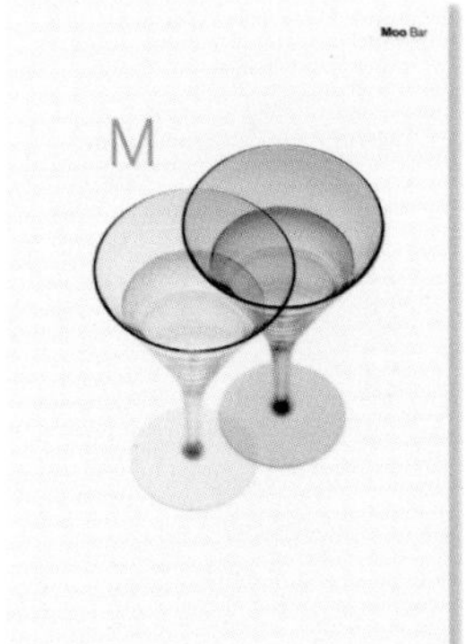
Moo Bar
M

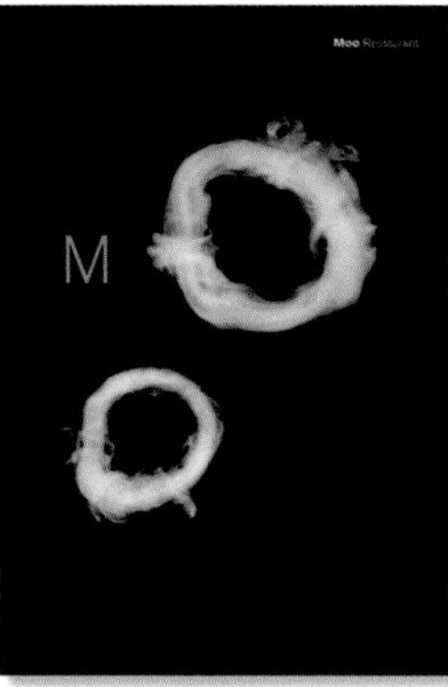
Moo Restaurant
M

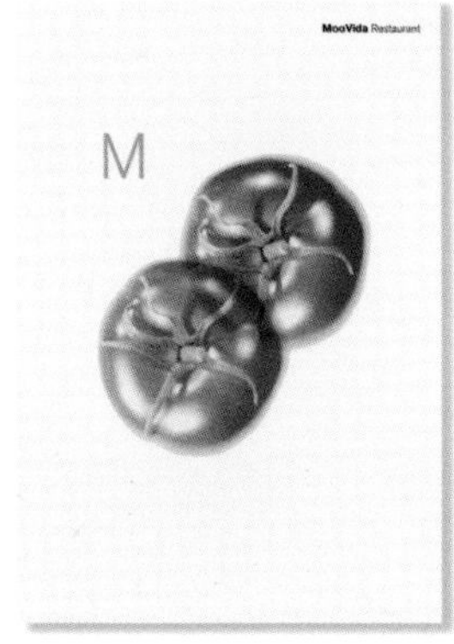
MooVida Restaurant
M

Moo
Moo

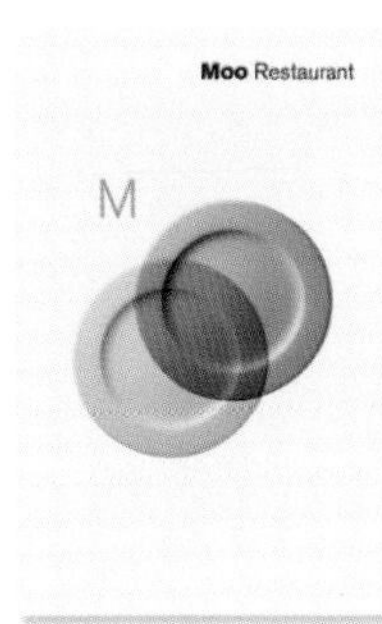
Moo Restaurant
M

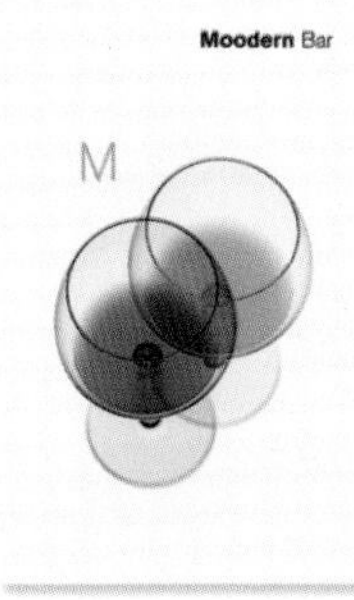
Moodern Bar
M

Charlar
Talk
Disfrutar
Drink
Comer
Look
Beure
Riure

OMMM

OMMSESSION

CLUB MÚSICA COPES CONCIERTOS
AMICS FRIENDS NIT DRINKS MUSIC
NOCHE DJ'S ESTIL ESPACIO LLUM
ESPAI LIGHT COPAS NIGHT AMIGOS
ESTILO LUZ STYLE ESPACE CONCERTS

Hotel Omm

Por favor haga mi habitación
Please make my room

Por favor no molestar
Please do not disturb

Pampero

Client: Ron Añejo Pampero
Designer: Ana Lourenço
Oporto, Portugal
www.cargocollective.com/blackphant

Ana Lourenço

Ana Lourenço

Ron Añejo
PAMPERO

Ana Lourenço

Logan

Client: Logan Wines
Studio: War Design
Chippendale, Australia
www.wardesign.com.au

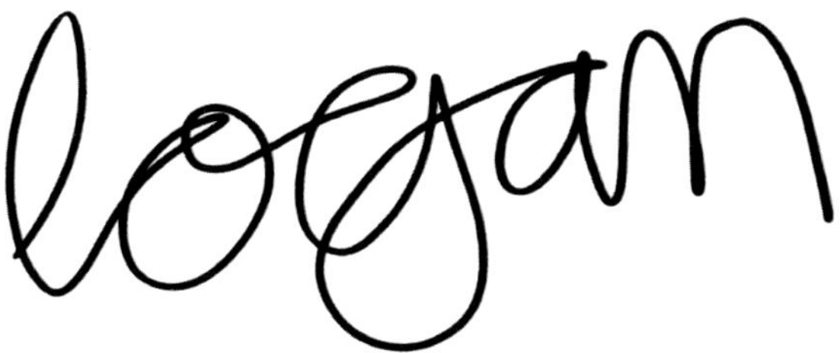

logan

logan
logan

logan
2007 Pinot Noir

logan

Logan

logan
2006 Cabernet Merlot
logan
2007 Pinot Noir
logan
2007 Chardonnay

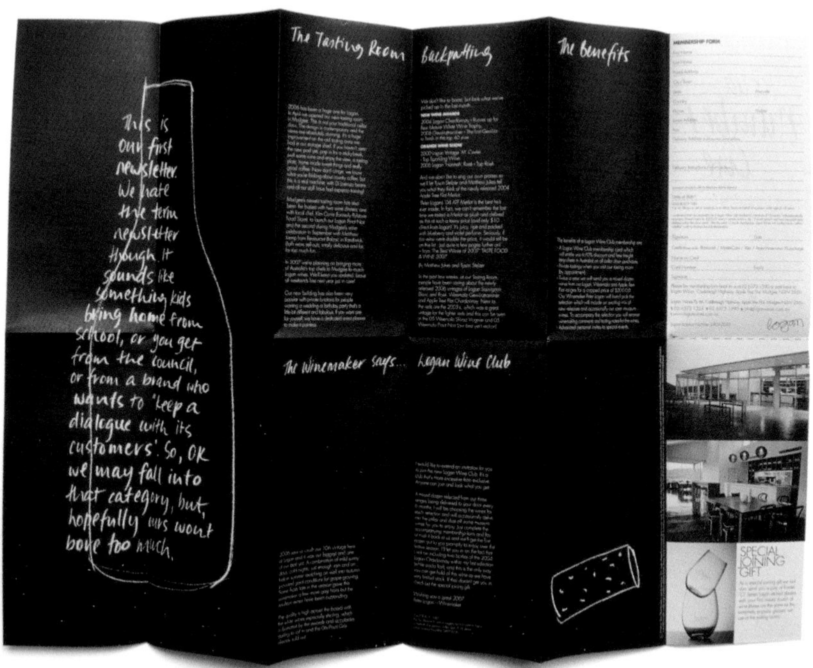
This is our first newsletter. We hate the term newsletter though. It sounds like something kids bring home from school, or you get from the council, or from a brand who wants to 'keep a dialogue with its customers'. So, OK we may fall into that category, but, hopefully ours won't bore too much.
The Tasting Room
Backpatting
The Benefits
The Winemaker says...
Logan Wine Club
MEMBERSHIP FORM
SPECIAL JOINING GIFT

Happywall

Client: Happywall cuadros y marcos
Studio: F33
Murcia, Spain
www.fundacion33.com

Sabadì

Client: Sabadì. Cioccolato di Modica
Studio: Happycentro
Designers: Federico Galvani, Andrea Manzati
Verona, Italy
www.happycentro.it

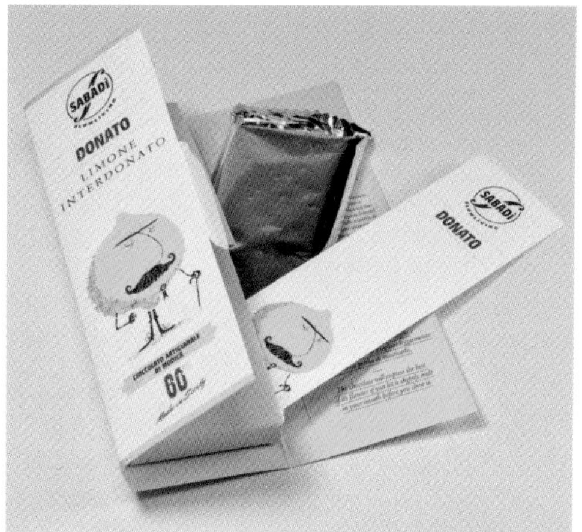

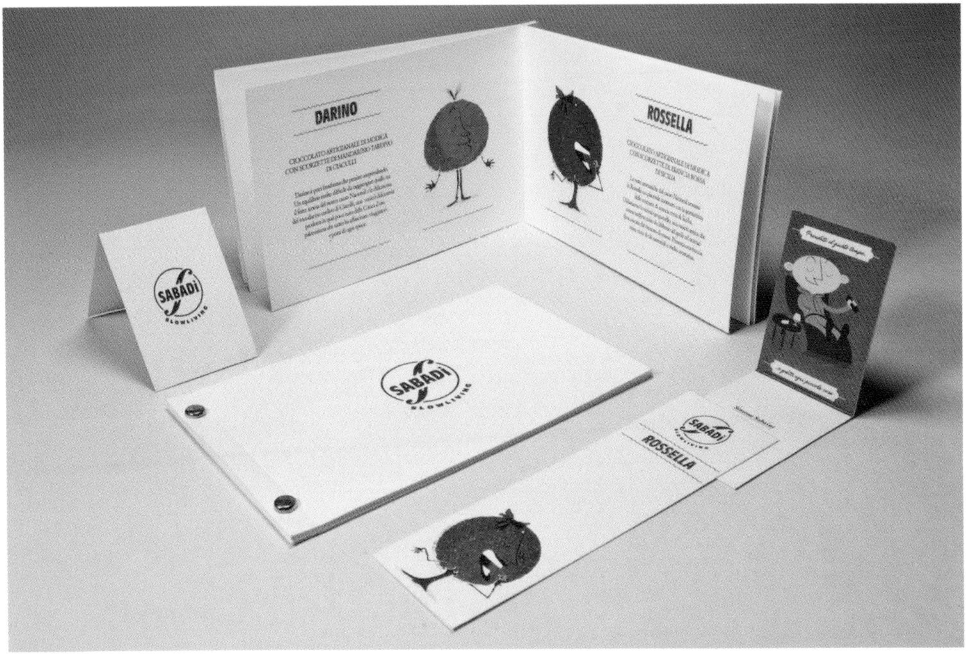
DARINO
ROSSELLA
SABADÌ
SLOWLIVING
SABADÌ
SLOWLIVING
SABADÌ
ROSSELLA

SABADÌ
SLOWLIVING
DONATO
LIMONE
INTERDONAT
CIOCCOLATO ARTIGIANALE
DI MODICA
60
Made in Sicily
SABADÌ
SLOWLIVING
DARINO
MANDARIN
TARDIVO
DI CIACULL
CIOCCOLATO ARTIGIANALE
50%
Made in Sicily
SABADÌ
SLOWLIVING
ROSSELLA
ARANCIA
ROSSA
CIOCCOLATO ARTIGIANALE
DI MODICA
60%
Made in Sicily
SABADÌ
SLOWLIVING
NELLA
CANNELLA
CIOCCOLATO ARTIGIANALE
DI MODICA
60%
Made in Sicily
SABADÌ
SLOWLIVING
LO SCURO
ZUCCHERO
MASCOBADO
ZUCCHERO MASCOBADO
CIOCCOLATO ARTIGIANALE
DI MODICA
70%
Made in Sicily
SABADÌ
SLOWLIVING
CINO
PEPERONCINO
PEPERONCINO
CIOCCOLATO ARTIGIANALE
DI MODICA
60%
Made in Sicily

Sabadì

PEPERONCINO
SLOWLIVING
CIOCCOLATO ARTIGIANALE DI MODICA
50%
Made in Sicily
CIOCCOLATO ARTIGIANALE DI MODICA
60%
Made in Sicily
CIOCCOLATO ARTIGIANALE DI MODICA
60%
Made in Sicily

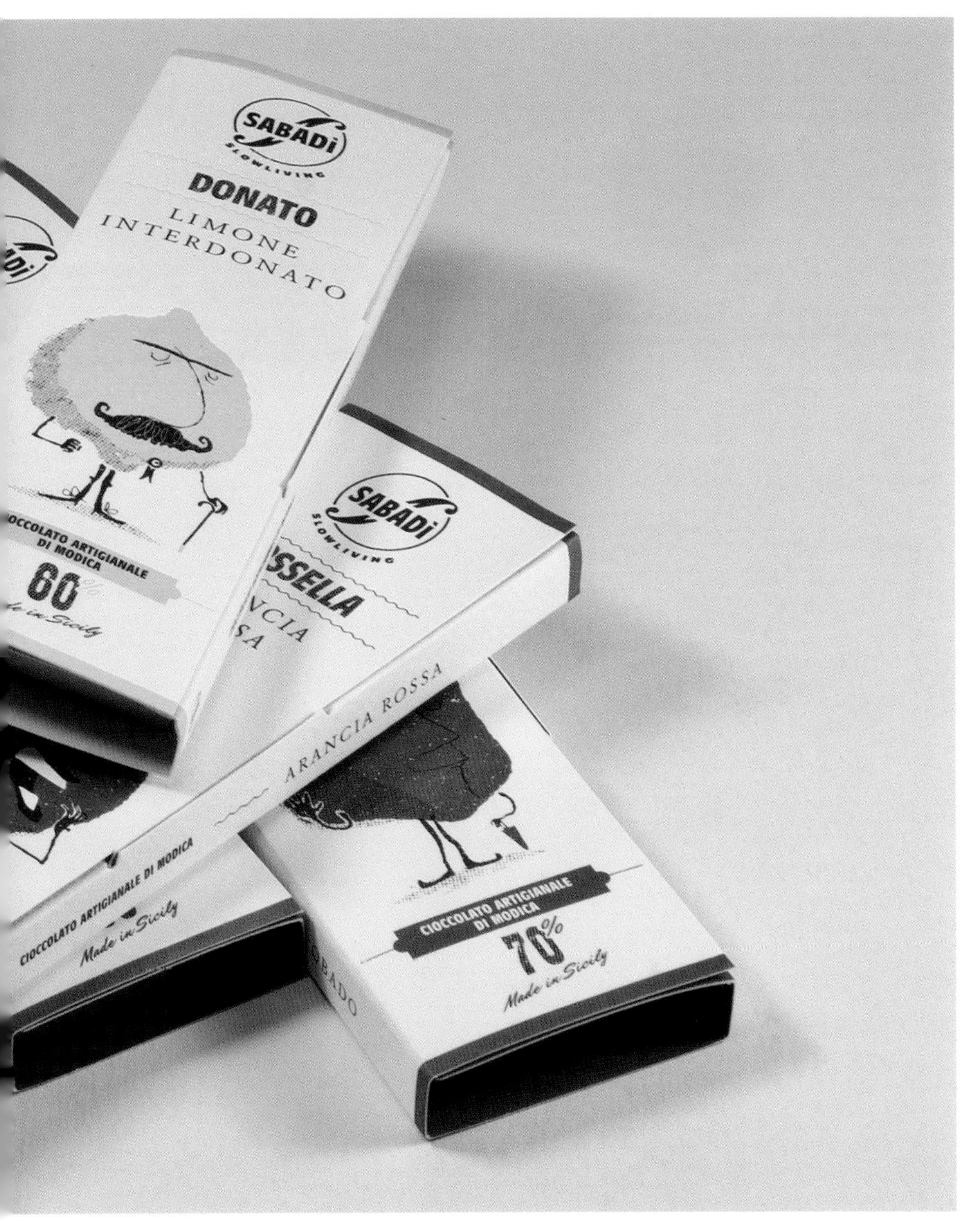
SABADì
SLOWLIVING
DONATO
LIMONE
INTERDONATO
CIOCCOLATO ARTIGIANALE
DI MODICA
60%
SABADì
SLOWLIVING
ARANCIA ROSSA
CIOCCOLATO ARTIGIANALE DI MODICA
Made in Sicily
CIOCCOLATO ARTIGIANALE
DI MODICA
70%
Made in Sicily

Directory Magazine

Client: Extreme Information
Studio: SVIDesign
Creative Director: Sasha Vidakovic
Designers: Sarah Bates, Kat Egerer
London, United Kingdom
www.svidesign.com

DIRECTORY
NEW IDEAS IN DIRECT MARKETING

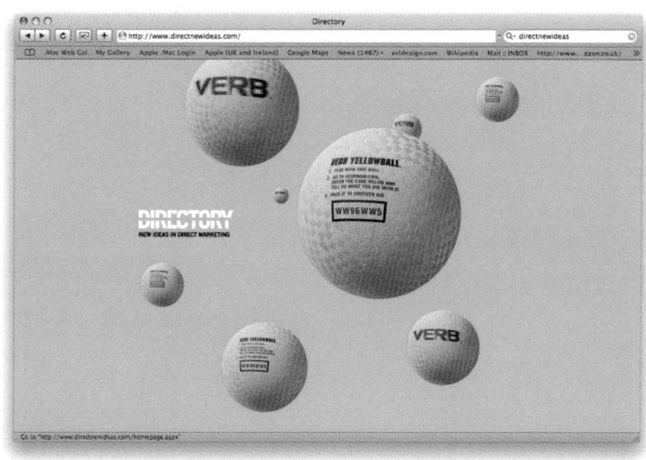

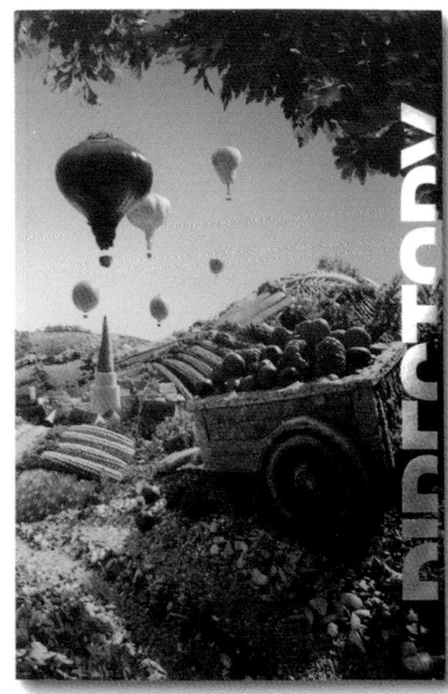

CLIENT
Tourism Australia

Product
Business Events

Title
Re-energise

Media
Mail, online, podcast, email

Country
Australia

Date
May 2007

BACKGROUND
Tourism Australia is tasked with promoting (and selling) Australia as a business conference and events destination. This is a complex task due to a highly competitive global environment for hosting events, where Australia is perceived to be a remote and costly option compared to new destinations such as Dubai and China. The sector is driven by 'relationships' that need to be nurtured in order to drive business. The objective was to generate and engage 25% of warm leads from all contacts mailed.

IDEA
Making any decision that costs the business money, and involves flying half way across the world, can be a difficult process. Even more so as the decision making process within large organisations often involves many different individuals. To make it easier, the agency's strategy was first to excite multiple contacts about Australia as a business events destination and then to provide them with the tools that would make it easy for them to make their event a reality. A multi-channel campaign with separate, but inter-related, pieces was developed, with each piece aimed at getting the right information about hosting events in Australia to the right recipient in the decision-making process. The 'Corporate Decision Maker', who is responsible for final sign-off but usually relies on somebody else to gather all the information and do the organising (the 'influencer'), was sent a pack intended to get them excited about Australia. It contained a specially commissioned, limited edition artwork by renowned Aboriginal artist Jimmy Nerrimah, on the theme of 'rejuvenation'.

The artwork came with a booklet that provided the recipient with top-line information about re-energising their business team in Australia. It also informed them that their colleague had received another pack supplying all the information needed for organising a conference in Australia. Influencers received a mail pack that resembled a didgeridoo. Each pack contained a special edition Events Australia iPod with a pre-loaded podcast showcasing Australia as a business event destination and inviting them to visit their personalised website. On the website, each visitor encountered a landing page specific to their company. They were invited to register to receive the Events Kit (a set of books) and ongoing case studies. As planning a large business event can take up to two years, this would ensure an ongoing dialogue. They were also able to forward the podcast to people within their company and these people were also encouraged to register to receive ongoing case studies.

RESULTS
The campaign delivered 46% of all recipients as warm leads with each of these recipients logging onto their personalised website, and either registering for an Events Kit (13%), subscribing to a podcast (17%), or contacting Tourism Australia personally to praise the campaign and express their thanks for the pack (18%). In addition to the people who directly received the packs, an average of six other people per company also logged onto the website. Furthermore, while most events are planned two years in advance, this campaign has already seen one confirmed booking and another in advanced planning for an event for 10,000 people each of which, according to research, will deliver AU$400 per person per day in spend.

EDITOR'S COMMENTS
If you're going to talk to top CEOs and get them to commit large sums of money to organising conferences in your country, you can't do it by halves. Once again it's the Australians who demonstrate that money spent on production is money well spent. Everything they mailed was something you'd want to keep if you were the recipient. And the first response – a company pledging to bring 10,000 people to Oz, each spending $400 a day. So that's upwards of $12m in additional revenue already. Spend money on production and you will be rewarded, truly. PC

AGENCY
M&C Saatchi / Mark, Australia

Creative team
Gavin McLeod
Creative Director
Shane Bradnick, Gavin McLeod
Art Directors
Dustin Lane, Dave King, George Shaw
Copywriters

Production
Josephine Panetta
Producer
Elly Gillis, Tammi Lukar
Online Producer

Other
Kimberlee Wells, Eleni Pelosi, Lara Wolski
Client Service

96 DIRECTORY 2007 Issue 5

97 DIRECTORY Integrated

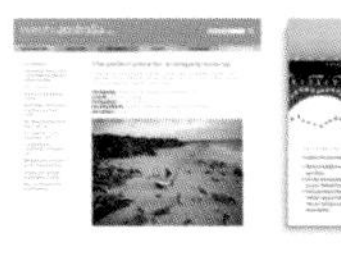

Directory Magazine

DIRECTORY

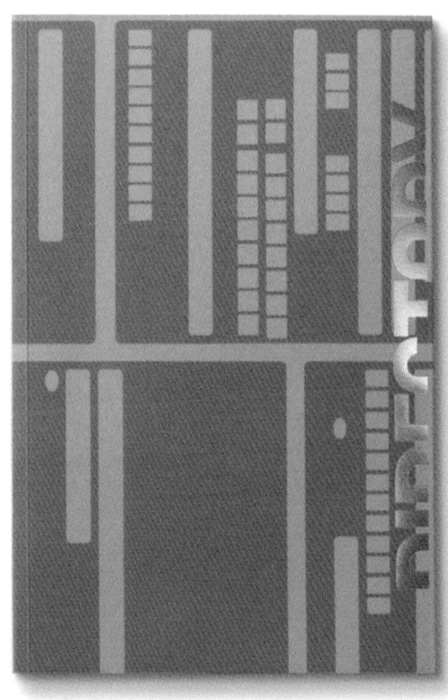
DIRECTORY

DIRECTORY

DIRECTORY

Copenhagen Parts

Client: Copenhagen Parts Bike Porter
Studio: Wolff Olins
Designer: Mads Jakob Poulsen
New York, USA
www.madsjakobpoulsen.dk

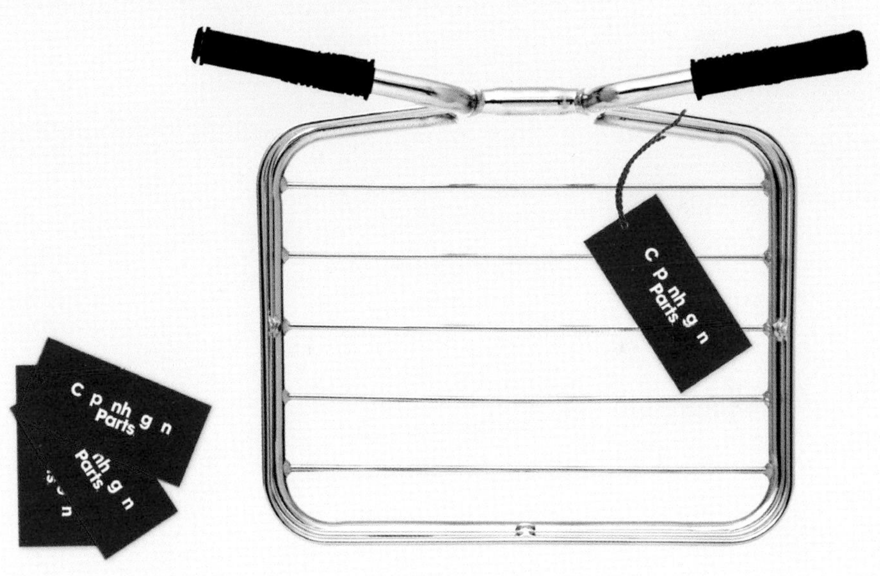
C P nh g n
Parts.

Copenhagen Parts

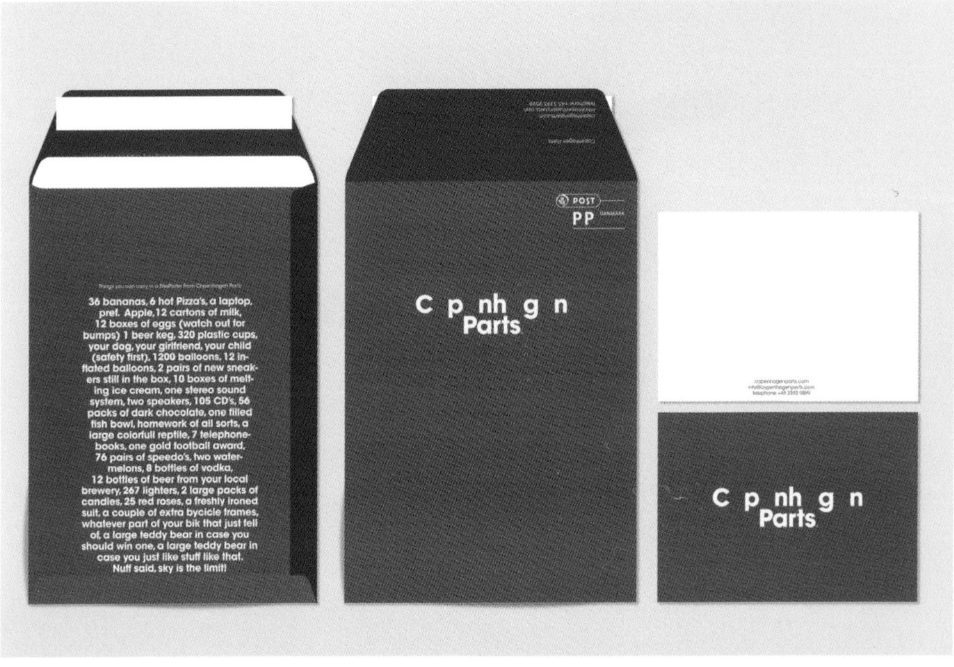

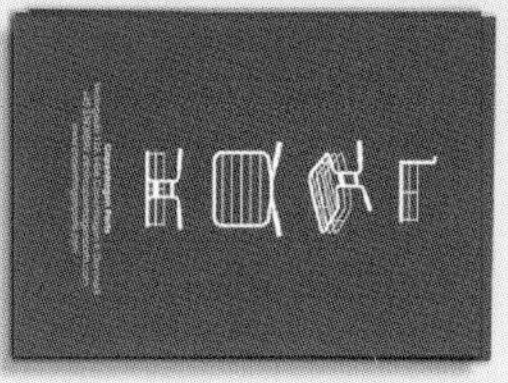

I+Drink

Client: I+Drink
Studio: m Barcelona
Designers: Marion Dönneweg & Merche Alcalá
Barcelona, Spain
www.m-m.es

I+Drink

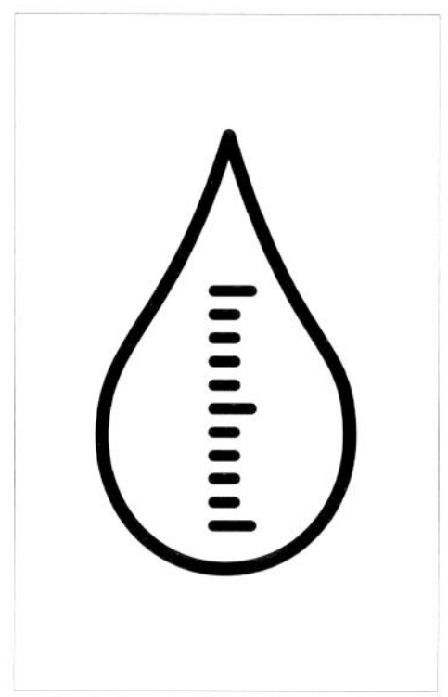

PABLO ALVAREZ
Director Financiero
e-mail: pabloalvarez@imasdrink.com
C: Fruela 3, 33007 Oviedo
T: +34 985 20 81 20
F: +34 985 20 81 40
W: www.imasdrink.com

PABLO ALVAREZ
Director Financiero
e-mail: pabloalvarez@imasdrink.com
C: Fruela 3, 33007 Oviedo
T: +34 985 20 81 20
F: +34 985 20 81 40
W: www.imasdrink.com

I+Love
I+Drink
I+Bordeaux
I+Lemon
I+E=Mc2
I+Sinatra
I+Santiago de Cuba
I+Lady Day
I+Tea
I+Drink
I+Strawberry
I+Moloko
I+John, Paul, George, Ringo
I+Drink
I+Mint
I+Shake

Nonell Restaurant

Client: Nonell Restaurant
Studio: Neil Cutler Design
Designer: Neil Cutler
Barcelona, Spain
www.neilcutler.com

nonell
Restaurant

Plaça Isidre Nonell
08002 Barcelona
Tel 93 301 1378

nonell
Restaurant

nonell
Restaurant

Plaça Isidre Nonell
Barcelona

Plaça Isidre Nonell 08002 Barcelona Tel 93 301 1378

DIRECTORY

Acosta Capeli A. Publi.
Argentina
www.acostacapelli.com.ar
pages: 12-13

Aleix Gordo Hostau
Spain
www.aleixgoho.com
pages: 8-11, 30-31

Ana Lourenço
Oporto, Portugal
www.cargocollective.com/blackphant
pages: 166-167

Barfutura
Spain
www.barfutura.com
pages: 130-133

Buch Design
United Kingdom / Croatia
www.bunchdesign.com
pages: 150-153

Carbone Smolan Agency
USA
www.carbonesmolan.com
pages: 26-27

Carrió Sánchez Lacasta
Spain
www.carriosanchezlacasta.com
pages: 148-149

Cherry Bomb Design Studio
Mexico
www.cherrybomb.com.mx
pages: 60-67

Cyla Costa
Brazil
www.behance.net/cylacosta
pages: 74-77

Department United Creative Forces
Switzerland
www.department.ch
pages: 20-23

Design Friendship
United Kingdom
www.designfriendship.com
pages: 126-127

Dima Je
Russian Federation
www.be.net/Dimaje
pages: 36-41

Dúctil
Spain
www.ductilct.com
pages: 107

Eduardo del Fraile
Spain
www.eduardodelfraile.com
pages: 32-33

Eric Chan
China
www.ericchandesign.com
pages: 94-95

F33
Spain
www.fundacion33.com
pages: 171

Form
United Kingdom
www.form.uk.com
pages: 52-53

Happycentro
Italy
www.happycentro.it
pages: 172-175

iDEOlab
Spain
www.ideolab.com
pages: 158-159

Inercia gráfica
Spain
www.inerciagrafica.com
pages: 78-79, 104-106, 136-139, 154-157

Jekyl & Hyde
Italy
www.jeh.it
pages: 28-29

Jonathan Calugi
Italy
www.behance.net/lovers
pages: 48-51

Leandro Dário
Brazil
www.leandrodario.com
pages: 98-99

Limón Studio
Mexico
www.cargocollective.com/limonestudio
pages: 42-43, 128-129

m Barcelona
Spain
www.m-m.es
pages: 44-46, 184-185

Mandala
Spain
www.mandaladgrafica.com
pages: 16-19

Marina Company
Spain
www.mirindacompany.com
pages: 108-112

Mario Eskenazi
Spain
www.m-eskenazi.com
pages: 100-102, 160-165

Mister Onüff
Spain
www.misteronuff.com
pages: 88-93

Neil Cutler Design
Spain
www.neilcutler.com
pages: 47, 186-187

No Visible Man Estudio
Spain
www.novisiblemanestudio.com
pages: 84-87

Puigdemont Roca Design Agency
Spain
www.puigdemontroca.com
pages: 14-15

Punto de Fuga
Argentina
www.puntodefuga.com.ar
pages: 72-73

Raymond Interactive
France
www.raymond-interactive.com
pages: 80-83

Rgb/Dg
Argentina
www.rgbdg.com.ar
pages: 124-125

Sergio Rey, María Ballesta
Spain
sergioreyazcona@gmail.com
m.ballesta@hotmail.com
pages: 96-97

Signun
Spain
www.signun.es
pages: 34-35

Shin Tanaka
USA
www.shin.co.nr
pages: 114-119

Sonsoles Llorens
Spain
www.sonsoles.com
pages: 140-143

Studio Snooze
Croatia
www.studiosnooze.com
pages: 120-121

SVIDesign
United Kingdom
www.svidesign.com
pages: 176-179

Tenfold Collective
USA
www.tenfoldcollective.com
pages: 113

The Luxury of Protest
United Kingdom
www.theluxuryofprotest.com
pages: 144-145

Turnstyle
USA
www.turnstylestudio.com
pages: 54-59, 122-123

Vit-e Design Studio
Lebanon
www.vit-e.com
pages: 24-25, 146-147

War Design
Australia
www.wardesign.com.au
pages: 168-170

Wolff Olins
USA
www.madsjakobpoulsen.dk
pages: 180-183

X-House Brand Consultant Agency
China
www.x-house.cn
pages: 68-71

Xosé Teiga
Spain
www.xoseteiga.com
pages: 103, 134-135

HERBAL
Lust for
PURIFYING
PURIFICANTE